Computers
in
Insurance

Computers
in
Insurance

ALAN J. TURNER, CPCU
JAMES GATZA, D.B.A., CPCU

Third Edition • 1990

AMERICAN INSTITUTE FOR
PROPERTY AND LIABILITY UNDERWRITERS
720 Providence Road, Malvern, Pennsylvania 19355-0770

Foreword

Over the years, the American Institute for Property and Liability Underwriters and the Insurance Institute of America have responded to the educational needs of the property and liability insurance industry by developing courses and administering national examinations specifically for insurance personnel. These independent, nonprofit educational organizations receive the support of the insurance industry in fulfilling this need.

The American Institute confers the Chartered Property Casualty Underwriter (CPCU®) professional designation on those who meet the experience, ethics, and examination requirements.

The Insurance Institute of America, founded in 1909, offers a wide range of associate designations and certificate programs in technical and managerial disciplines.

Accredited Adviser in Insurance (AAI®)
Associate in Claims (AIC)
Associate in Underwriting (AU)
Associate in Risk Management (ARM)
Associate in Loss Control Management (ALCM®)
Associate in Premium Auditing (APA®)
Associate in Management (AIM)
Associate in Research and Planning (ARP®)
Associate in Insurance Accounting and Finance (AIAF)
Associate in Automation Management (AAM®)
Associate in Marine Insurance Management (AMIM®)
Associate in Reinsurance (ARe)
Certificate in General Insurance
Certificate in Supervisory Management
Certificate in Introduction to Claims
Certificate in Introduction to Property and Liability Insurance

This text is used in five Institute programs: the Chartered Property Casualty Underwriter program, the Associate in Management program, the Associate in Insurance Accounting and Finance program, the Associate in Loss Control Management program, and the Associate in Marine Insurance Management program. In each of these programs, *Computers in Insurance* meets the need for a brief summary of automation and its use in insurance information systems. In essence, this book provides highlights. Those who want an in-depth treatment of insurance automation are urged to obtain information on the Associate in Automation Management (AAM) program from the Institutes.

As with all Institute publications, this text has been extensively reviewed by a group of academic and industry experts, and they are recognized in the preface. Throughout the development of this series of texts, it has been—and will continue to be—necessary to draw on the knowledge and skills of Institute personnel. These individuals receive no royalties on texts sold; their writing responsibilities are seen as an integral part of their professional duties. We have proceeded in this way to avoid any possibility of conflict of interests.

We invite and welcome any and all criticisms of our publications. It is only with such comments that we can hope to provide high quality study materials. Comments should be directed to the Curriculum Department of the Institutes.

Norman A. Baglini, Ph.D., CPCU, CLU
President and Chief Executive Officer

Preface

Undeniably, automation is a major force in our lives: it seems to reach every cranny. We see computers virtually everywhere in virtually all property and liability insurance organizations. It might seem that computers, as a famous song says about the people in Kansas City, "have gone about as far as they can go." Not so. There is no end in sight to the parade of new features, new applications, and improvements to old applications. Insurance automation is a servant whose muscles and whose reach keep growing.

This is the third edition of *Computers in Insurance*. Like its predecessors, it is shaped by the learning objectives of CPCU 7, the CPCU management course, and other Institute courses. It is designed to meet the educational need for three assignments on insurance automation in courses primarily devoted to other subjects. This book focuses on the role of automation in insurance organizations and on key issues in the management of computers and information systems. Those who seek a broader treatment and want to build skill in using and managing automated resources are advised to take the Insurance Institute of America's Associate in Automation Management program.

As with all Institute texts, outside reviewers contributed significantly to the final product. We appreciate the substantial contributions made by those who reviewed this third edition:

Wayne H. Bossov, CPCU, ARM, AAM
Zurich-American Insurance Group

John C. Stiegler
Safeco Insurance Companies

Dr. Michael W. Varano
Villanova University

Karl A. Waite, CPCU, ARM, AIAF, CDP
Central Insurance Companies

With authors, as with technology, things change. The first edition of this book was written in large part by Michael D. Gantt, CPCU. Mike Gantt entered the ministry shortly after completing his work on the text—no connection is implied—and Rev. Michael D. Gantt did not assist in writing the second or this third edition. Nonetheless, his contributions endure. Alan J. Turner, CPCU, became involved as primary author of the second edition. He continued in this role despite the increasing responsibilities of his work. As the Institute staff member involved, it has been my privilege to work with these highly talented and dedicated individuals.

As insurance automation continues to evolve, so too must this text. Your critical comments and suggestions will be welcomed.

James Gatza, D.B.A., CPCU
Vice President
American Institute for
Property and Liability Underwriters

Table of Contents

CHAPTER 1

The Computer

Automation is the paramount tool for doing insurance work. In companies, agencies, and brokerage firms alike, nearly every desk has a computer or computer terminal. In one sense, the campaign is over—the insurance industry has been automated for many years. In another sense, the campaign continues as automation is asked to conquer new areas and to perform new duties. This latter notion is the more fruitful one, since the process of automating or improving the automation of insurance tasks is ongoing. It follows, then, that those who perform, supervise, or manage insurance work should have a working knowledge of the automation resource.

This text surveys the expanding field of insurance automation. It contains *descriptive* material on how computers work, how insurance firms are automated, and how insurance organizations exchange information through automated interface. This text also contains ideas on how automation is and should be managed in insurance organizations. Thus it offers both *descriptive* and *prescriptive* material on the management of automation and automated work. Throughout, it views automation as an unending process and a resource of enormous potential for the insurance organization. It presumes that you want to understand and make better use of that resource.

BASIC CONCEPTS

Defining the Computer

What is a computer? The American National Standards Institute offers this definition:

> Computer—a data processor that can perform computation, including numerous arithmetic or logic operations, without intervention by a human operator during the run.[1]

Unfortunately, this definition raises more questions than it answers. It will be useful to think of a data processor as a type of machine and a run as the sequence of computational steps to be performed on the data. The word *program* denotes the instructions for the run or, loosely, the run itself.

A computer, therefore, can be distinguished from other information-handling machines (such as adding machines) by its ability to hold an *internally stored program* (a sequence of computational steps). It is the internally stored program, or instructions for a run, that eliminates the need for intervention by a human operator during that run.

An adding machine is *not* a computer because each calculation requires human intervention To rate an automobile policy using an adding machine, for example, it is necessary to take the machine through a sequence of steps. It is not possible simply to type the required rating factors and hit a key telling the adding machine to "rate" the policy. The adding machine cannot "remember" formulas. With the internally stored program, a computer can "remember" the steps to take in the rating formula.

It might be worthwhile to note that many of the electronic calculators now on the market are computers, since they can be "programmed" to perform specified operations. Their capabilities are severely limited when compared with business computers but they do demonstrate that "size does not a computer make." A computer is not restricted to any particular shape or size.

Adding to the confusion is the fact that numerous different terms are used for the computer field. These include, but are not limited to: *automatic data processing (ADP)*, *electronic data processing (EDP)*, *data processing (DP)*, *management information systems (MIS)*, and *information systems (IS)*. Although textbook authors have tried to maintain specific and slightly different definitions for these terms, most people in the business world use them almost interchangeably. The term *computer science* may be one exception to this. Although this term also refers to the field of computers, its use has been restricted to the study of computers and their operation as opposed to the management of them in business organizations.

The rapid increase in capabilities and the widespread distribution of computers have contributed to the semantic tangle. Definitions can suddenly become obsolete with the development of new equipment or concepts.

Types of Computers [2]

It is possible to classify computers in many ways. In this section, we will use three approaches for classification.

Analog or Digital. Analog computers are those that measure continuously variable data. The name analog comes from the fact that measurements recorded are "analogous" to the actual data in question. This is best shown by example. One of the most common examples is the speedometer in an automobile. The pointer represents the rotational motion of the drive shaft. The miles per hour figure, therefore, is analogous to the rotation of the drive shaft. Where the need exists for continuous, or constant, measurement of some process or quantity, analog computers work best.

Digital computers perform computation on noncontinuous, discrete data; that is, they use digits. They measure only in the sense that they count in exact figures. For example, if a computer is to add up the total amount of money received by a business in a day, a digital computer would be used. The computer would add up all the individual receipts and arrive at a discrete answer (for example, $1,080.22). It is now impossible to shop for a wristwatch without confronting the choice between the traditional analog kind (with hands that move continuously) and digital-reading models.

Although analog computers are sometimes used in business (mainly in building maintenance systems), they are primarily used for scientific purposes. Obviously, most insurance organization computers are digital computers

Special Purpose or General Purpose. A digital computer can be designed as a special purpose or general purpose machine. As you might expect, the *special purpose computer* is designed with one specific function in mind. Because of this, the special purpose computer can perform its task in an extremely efficient manner. Its disadvantage is, of course, that it can fulfill no purpose other than the one for which it was designed. For example, some fast food restaurants have computerized cash registers. Each item on the menu has a corresponding button on the register. These machines speed customer service, reduce arithmetic errors, control inventories, and perform other functions. They do these things well, but are useless for other applications.

The *general purpose computer* can perform many different tasks or functions by running many different programs. It is not as efficient as a special purpose computer performing its given task in the same way that an all-purpose cleaner is not likely to clean glass as well as a glass cleaner. Its prime virtue lies in its flexibility. It is this flexibility that makes the computer economical in many cases. It is unlikely that an insurance agency would dedicate one computer for printing policies, another for collecting payments, and yet another for payroll, since a personal computer can be programmed to handle all of these tasks. Obviously, then, the general purpose computer is the dominant one in insurance industry installations.

Scientific Use or Business Use. Computer design requirements for scientific usage differ in nature from those for business usage. A little reflection will reveal some of the major differences. A scientific user, who may not actually be a scientist, is frequently concerned with formulas and simulations of the real world. Scientific work can involve hundreds, even thousands, of complex calculations or slight alterations to a basic formula. Computers can take the drudgery out of these and other tasks by performing many repetitive computations for the researcher. The researcher is probably not going to be interested in documenting a large number of intermediate calculations. The researcher will be interested in the final results. Some examples of scientific uses in the insurance industry are developing rates, evaluating loss reserves, and the construction of computer models for planning.

Conversely, business uses generally require little in the way of sophisticated computation but a great deal of input and output. Policyholder billing, for example, requires calculation of the amount owed and printing of a bill. No calculus or geometry is required—just a little arithmetic and a great deal of printing.

This text will concentrate on digital, general purpose, business-use computers. Discussion now turns to the mechanical processes performed by or within a computer. In a mechanical sense, the computer reads, stores, and writes information. It also performs calculations, and it controls these operations as it performs them.

Data Representation

Data and information are both raw materials and products of computers. In this sense, the computer reminds people of themselves (though, it is hoped, not in any other sense). People collect information, process it, and come up with some result. The computer, however, is unable to read a book, at least in the way people read. It is unable to view a sunset or hear a symphony. In short, the ways in which it can collect information are extremely limited. Although many different types of devices exist to collect information for the computer, they must reduce that information to a particular form, *binary form*. Within the computer, each individual circuit can be in only one of two states. That is, each circuit is either on or off, positive or negative—no other possibilities exist. This might seem like a very limited arrangement; but in fact, it is quite effective.[3]

All data (numbers, letters, and special characters contained on a computer keyboard) are represented in this binary manner within the computer. Universal product codes on items purchased at grocery stores are read by the computer in this way. A scanner at the checkout counter "looks" for the series of lines or bars making up the code. Depending on the thickness and sequence of bars, a binary value for each number making up the universal product code is derived. All data are built up from individual binary values. A particular circuit in the computer represents a *bit* (short for binary digit) by being on or off. Decimal numbers and letters of the alphabet are represented by specific combinations of bits, called *bytes*. For example, CPCU is represented as 11000011 11010111 11000011 11100100 when stored in binary form by large IBM mainframe computers. All data must exist in this binary form before the computer can perform any calculations or even store the data.

Once the form data must take within the computer is known, it is possible to look at the basic functions performed by the computer.[4] Keep in mind that only professional systems programmers work with binary representation of data, and even then, infrequently. Most programming is done in the words and commands of specific programming languages that are later converted (by the computer) into binary form.

Computer Functions

The actual mechanical tasks performed by a computer involve five major functions. A computer reads, writes, and stores data, performs calculations, and controls these operations as it performs them.

Read (Input). A computer reads data in order to begin solving problems. In fact, the computer must also read in the program (program instructions are just another form, albeit a special one, of data) that prescribes the operations to be performed. Computer terminals, disk and tape drives, and other devices are used to collect or read information. Regardless of the device, the information reaches the computer in binary representation. Information read by the computer is called, of course, input.

Write (Output). When the computer has finished processing a given input, it will write or produce the output. Various devices are used for the output function. The printer and computer terminal are the most familiar, but output does not have to be in humanly readable form. The output, for example, could be written to a magnetic tape, floppy disk, or placed on a hard disk to be input later for another computer operation.

Store (Storage). A computer must store information until needed. Recall the definition of a computer. It is the ability to store that differentiates a computer from other information-handling machines. The computer has the capability to store a sequence of computational steps (i.e., an internally stored program) as well as the ability to store data for computation.

Calculate. Once data and instructions have been read and stored by the computer and before the answer can be written, the answer must be calculated. This may be either an *arithmetic operation* (1 + 1 = ?) or *logic operation* (is 5 greater than 4?). Computers add, subtract, multiply, divide, and perform any formulas provided in the form of instructions. They also perform logical comparisons between values (for example, logical comparisons are repetitively performed when the computer "sorts" lists into alphabetical order).

Control. This last major function of the computer has been implicit in the discussion of all the others. The operations of reading, writing, storing, and calculating must be controlled. There must be order in the machine or else it will begin to read when it should write or store when it should calculate. Some of this control is designed into the circuits of the computer, while the rest is provided by the instructions in the programs run on the computer.

Components of the Computer System [5]

The computer system is a collection of three elements: hardware, software, and people.

Hardware. The term hardware refers to the physical devices, including the computer itself. The *central processing unit* (CPU) is the heart of the computer system. It is here that all control and calculation functions take place. Input and output devices are also considered hardware. Input and output devices are contained in the same "box" as the CPU or connected to it by cable. The CPU delegates the reading and writing of data to the input and output machines. In addition to these machines, there are supporting devices that are attached to these machines and perform various "housekeeping" functions for the primary devices already mentioned. We will study all of these in greater detail later in this chapter.

Software. A stored program is the set of instructions that tell a computer what steps to take and in what order to take them. It also tells the computer what data to read, and, at the proper time, what data to write. The term *software* includes all the programs used to run the computer. These instructional programs can be divided into two categories. Programs used to perform operations necessary to the basic operation of the computer are called *system software*. Perhaps the most important part of system software is the *operating system*, which makes the hardware work. For example, PC-DOS and MS-DOS are the names of operating systems used in an IBM and IBM compatible personal computer. MVS/XA is the name of an operating system used by large IBM mainframe computers. Programs applying to specific problems being processed in the computer are called *application software*. Lotus 1-2-3 is the name of a popular personal computer application software program.

In an insurance company, programs dealing with insurance matters and company matters are considered application software. System software includes programs dealing with the operation of the computer itself which are scarcely known beyond the confines of the data processing department or system vendor.

Capabilities [6]

It is important to have a conceptual understanding of what computers can and cannot do in order to make decisions that lead to efficient use of computers. What are the specific capabilities of computers?

Handle Large Volume of Repetitive Tasks Accurately. Much of the work that goes on in today's insurance organization is repetitive paper work. A computer can perform most of these tasks much faster than a human being can and with far fewer errors (if it is programmed correctly). The computer, fortunately, does not get "bored" with all this repetition or become fatigued by it.

Process Jobs Almost Simultaneously. This feature is referred to as *multiprogramming*. The computer does not need to complete one job before starting another. While the computer is *reading* for one program, it might be *writing* for another, and *calculating* for a third.

Although the computer can calculate for only one job at a time, control switches back and forth so fast (in nanoseconds—a nanosecond is one thousandth of a millionth of a second) that it appears to us that the jobs are being processed simultaneously—hence the phrase "almost simultaneously." "Almost simultaneous" processing of jobs is possible because some computer functions are performed faster than others. For example, computers can calculate much faster than they can read or write. Multiprogramming allows many calculations to take place while the essentially slower process of reading goes on.

Multiprocessing is another way of reducing computing time. Instead of having just one computer or processor as in multiprogramming, there are two or more computers or microprocessors in a multiprocessing system. One of the processors controls the operations of the others, which handle specialized tasks such as arithmetic calculations or filing and retrieving data.

Make Decisions. Computers are said to make decisions in a very limited sense. The computer has the ability to follow stored instructions, make a logical comparison, and then based on that comparison take a specified course of action. Computer programs frequently check the validity of data coming in and reject data that is not valid for reentry through a terminal at the time the error is made or suspends the invalid data for correction the next day. For example, if a computer program expects to read a policyholder file in order to print a listing of all policyholders with property in Alaska, the program should reject the input file if it turns out that somebody fed in a payroll file rather than a policyholder file. The limitation is that the computer can only make the decisions it has been programmed to make.

Perform Calculations—Arithmetic and Logic Functions. The computer is well known for its ability to add, subtract, multiply, and divide. Additionally, it can determine whether a number is positive, negative, or zero. It can also compare two quantities and determine whether one is larger, smaller, or if they are equal. After performing this logical comparison it can then *branch*, or *go to*, another part of the program. It can *go to* one of a series of operations based on the result of the logical comparison. (It is this ability that allows the computer to perform "decision-making" operations.)

Customer billing can illustrate how this branching logic operates. As each policyholder's records are read, a check is made of the current account balance. The logic might be as follows:

> Compare account balance to zero.
> If equal, go to next policyholder record.
> If greater than zero, go to billing routine.
> If less than zero, go to refund routine.

Remote Processing.   With the advent of telecommunications (transmitting data over telephone lines), computers have gained the ability to overcome their geographical limitations. A mainframe computer can have input and output devices hundreds or thousands of miles away. For instance, an insurer's home office computer might be connected with that of its claim representative in Spain, with the desktop terminal or personal computer of an agent in Miami, and with a medium-size computer in its Dallas branch.

Limitations [7]

The dissimilarities between a computer and a human being are far more striking than the similarities, although it is possible to get the opposite impression from reading some of the current literature on the subject. In fact, it sometimes sounds as if it were only a matter of time (however long) before computers have intelligence capabilities, that is, before they can carry on all the thinking processes of a human. Proper analysis of computer limitations will, however, dispel this notion.

Unable to Handle Anything Other Than Certain Quantitative, Logical Considerations.   The computer is not going to be able to figure out how the insurance executive should react to consumer interest groups, nor how the underwriting manager should train underwriters, nor how the claims examiner should handle a denial of coverage. Computer programs can act as consultants to underwriters in reviewing an application and to risk managers in interpreting insureds' needs and designing a complete risk management program, but they cannot replace these professionals.

For one thing, computers are amoral. Good and bad do not compute. Nor can computers "shoot from the hip," or use intuition as people must do at times in the business world. Computers cannot be inconsistent in their actions, and yet humans often want the inconsistency of a supervisor who bends the rules from time to time.

Does Only What It Is Programmed To Do.   Not only is the computer limited in the type of problem it can handle; it is further limited by its inability to do anything it has not been programmed to do.

For example, an agency's computer will accept a four-digit zip code if it has not been programmed to reject zip codes that are not five or nine digits.

The fantastic speed of the computer is a two-edged sword. Just as it can print insurance policies many times faster than a typist can, it can also, once it is programmed incorrectly, produce inaccurate policies many times faster than typists can. Does this mean that the programmer's error is more "wrong" than the typist's? Of course not. But the consequences of the programmer's error are far greater.

Economic Limitations.   Computers are further limited in the sense that, economically speaking, they should be used only to perform functions that would be more expensive to perform by other means. If a monthly expense account takes an executive ten minutes to total, while the computer would only take 18.753 nanoseconds, it does not follow that the executive should use the computer to add the expense account. The actual computation time of a program is a small part of the total time involved—including the time to write the program, to test the program, to set up the program to run, and most importantly, the time to input data. Computers should be used on those tasks that will meet the organization's business objectives and enhance the productivity of its employees.

COMPUTER HARDWARE

The Central Processor and Memory [8]

Central Processing Unit.   The CPU, sometimes called the mainframe or the processor, is the hub of all activity in the computer system. All calculations are performed by the CPU, and no machine in the system operates except under the control of the CPU. Input devices are used to read data. Output devices are used to write data. It is the central processing unit, however, which actually processes (performs calculations and controls) data.

Arithmetic/Logic Unit (ALU).   Before a calculation is made, data is transferred from primary storage to the *arithmetic/logic unit* and the calculation is performed. After the calculation is completed, the answer is transferred to primary storage. If this sounds like some sort of "musical data" game in which the CPU spends a great deal of time moving data back and forth from one section to another, remember that the computer is very limited in its functions (it can add, subtract, multiply, divide, and compare numbers). Everything must take place according to an ordered sequence. The speed at which the computer operates more than makes up for the seemingly cumbersome and rigid internal sequence it must follow.

Control Unit. If the CPU is the heart of the computer system, then the *control unit* is the heart of the central processing unit. It controls the calculations and other activities of the CPU and, therefore, of the computer system as a whole. The control unit receives and interprets program instructions from primary storage. Based on the instructions, the control unit will issue commands to the appropriate part of the computer system to initiate and direct the appropriate sequence of operations.

Primary Storage Unit. The *primary storage unit* of the CPU, as its name implies, stores data. Specifically, it stores instructions and data that are of immediate importance to the job being run. Primary storage differs from secondary storage (e.g., magnetic disk, discussed under input/output devices) in that it resides in the CPU and contains only data pertinent to the program currently being run.

Other terms for this storage include *internal memory, temporary memory, main memory, random access memory (RAM)* or *core.* Main memory must be distinguished from *auxiliary memory* or *auxiliary storage,* terms referring to *media* that will be discussed below. The term core comes from the fact that historically computer storage in many computers consisted of magnetic cores of iron oxide. Integrated circuits have all but replaced magnetic cores for main memory.

Types of Primary Storage. As noted earlier, data is represented in the computer in a binary state (either on or off, positive or negative). The particular physical device used in the computer to represent this binary state varies by computer and is determined primarily by cost factors. A number of devices have been used over the years. For example, some of the earliest electronic computers developed in the late 1940s and early 1950s used vacuum tubes for primary storage. By today's standards, these were too large, switched on and off too slowly, and were too expensive to make large computers cost effective in many business applications.

Magnetic Core. Earliest digital memories used *magnetic core* as the medium for primary storage. A single magnetic core is a tiny doughnut-shaped ring of iron ferrite, that was magnetized clockwise or counter clockwise, on or off at any one moment, to represent a bit of information. The CPU contained millions of these tiny rings, strung together by wiring. The magnetic core was a major improvement over vacuum tubes, but far more dramatic developments were still to come.

Semiconductor Memory.   Many of the computers produced today utilize *semiconductor memory.* Semiconductor circuits are etched in silicon chips. In one of these chips (about an eighth of an inch in area), over 256,000 binary digits can be stored. Semiconductor memory has all but replaced magnetic core for main storage because of its low cost, size, increased speed, and storage capacity. Third and fourth generation computers use integrated circuits produced by using large scale integration (LSI) and very large scale integration (VLSI) technologies for memories.

Storage Structure.   The primary storage unit of the CPU is divided into four areas: *program storage, input storage, output storage,* and *working storage.*

Program storage is where the computer stores the instructions for the program it is currently executing. The program must be represented within the computer in the same manner (binary code) as data. Input storage is the place where data is stored immediately after being read into the system by an input device. Output storage is where data is stored immediately before it is to be written by an output device. Working storage is where partially processed data is stored. The relative size of these four areas can be altered and controlled by the programmer. *Addressing* informs the computer where each of the four major storage areas starts and stops.

Bits, Bytes, and Words.   Each zero or one in a computer circuit represents a *bit.* Bits are combined to form a *byte,* the smallest unit in a computer capable of representing a letter, number, or any other special character present on a computer terminal keyboard. When a character is typed on the keyboard, a byte with a specific bit pattern is electronically transferred into memory. The specific bit pattern transferred depends on the particular coding structure used by the computer. Bytes are combined to form a *word.* Microcomputers typically use word lengths of two bytes, or sixteen bits; most mainframes and an increasing number of micros use four bytes or thirty-two bits. The larger supercomputers use word lengths of eight bytes or larger. Some manufacturers use other terms, but bit, byte, and word are standard in the insurance industry.

The central processing unit, then, is the center of activity in the computer system. From its control unit, all functions of the system are directed. In its arithmetic/logic unit, all calculations and logic comparisons are performed. Its primary storage unit holds all data currently being utilized, in core or RAM. Data is located within primary storage in major storage subdivisions. Individual pieces of information, that is, bits, bytes, or words of data are located within the CPU by the addressing procedure.

Permanent Storage. Primary storage provides the CPU with extremely fast access to data and program instructions. The cost of primary storage makes it too expensive for storing data and programs when they are not being used; therefore, other devices are required to store the programs and data on a permanent basis. The devices used to do this are called *auxiliary* or *permanent storage*. Although it takes the CPU longer to retrieve data and programs from them, permanent storage devices are much less expensive when compared to the cost of purchasing the same amount of primary storage. There are two categories of permanent storage devices.

Sequential access storage devices read and write data one record after another in a predetermined sequence such as customer, policy, or claim number. Tape drives and card readers are examples of sequential access storage devices. *Direct access storage devices (DASD)* permit the immediate reading and writing of data required within a few seconds, rather than starting at the beginning of the file and spinning through it until the desired record is found. An insurance agency's online system would not respond very quickly if the programs had to start at the beginning of the customer master file every time information on a customer was required.

Input/Output Devices [9]

Input devices allow computers to read information; output devices allow computers to write information. These devices are usually physically separate from the central processing unit, although they are connected by a cable through which digital signals pass back and forth. Today, *computer* generally refers to the CPU, input/output devices, and supporting devices in total. To think of the CPU as a computer would be equivalent to thinking of the human heart as a person.

The following list of devices is by no means exhaustive. It does, however, include those devices most likely to be encountered in the insurance industry.

Dedicated Data Entry Systems (I). A keyboard that transfers human readable data directly to magnetic tape or disks is a popular method of performing high volume data entry. Data from a source document is entered through a keyboard, checked for errors, and formatted into the sequence expected by the computer programs that will use the data as input.

Terminals (I/O). Terminals are devices that allow the users of a computer system to gain access to (that is, to input programs and data to, and to obtain output from) the system in a manner that standard input/output devices, such as disk drives and printers, will not allow. What this most often means is that while standard I/O devices must be close to the CPU, terminals can be almost anywhere. There must be a cable or communication link between the CPU and the terminal. Telephone line hook-ups can be either *dial-up* or *dedicated.* A dedicated or *leased* line is a permanent line installed between the computer and the terminal, eliminating the need for dialing. The two basic types of terminals are batch terminals and interactive terminals.

Batch Terminals (I/O). *Batch terminals* are used in much the same way that standard I/O devices are used at the computer site. They are particularly useful when many people wish to use the computer and yet are located at a distance from it. Service bureaus, companies that process data for their clients, use this approach to provide accounting services to insurance agencies. The service bureau places a terminal in the agency which is connected to the service bureau by telephone lines. Accounting information is then entered into the terminal and stored in the terminal's memory or on a floppy disk until it is sent to the service bureau all at once. A batch terminal may resemble a typewriter—it need not have a screen.

Interactive Terminals (I/O). *Interactive terminals* differ from batch terminals in that the user does not submit an entire task or series of tasks when using an interactive terminal. Instead, the user enters requests, including program instructions or data, one item at a time. The user receives a response before entering the next statement or request, hence the term interactive. (Sometimes the term *conversational* is used to describe the same characteristic.) Terminals are often classified as intelligent or dumb terminals. An *intelligent terminal* provides the user with data processing capabilities to manipulate data, in addition to serving as an input/output device. A personal computer used as a terminal is an intelligent terminal. *Dumb terminals*, such as those commonly connected to mainframes, are limited to input/output; they do not store or process data internally.

Another way of distinguishing terminals from other input/output devices is that terminals are usually described as *remote* I/O while other I/O devices are local. Although terminals are being used more and more as high-volume data entry or input devices, they can also be used to view low volumes of output. Other I/O devices are designed for high volumes. Since equipment terminology is used rather loosely, it is necessary to be specific when describing hardware items.

Interactive terminals are often referred to as *cathode-ray tubes (CRTs)* or *video display terminals (VDTs)*. CRTs are located in almost every area of insurance organizations. CRTs come in many shapes and sizes and are produced by many manufacturers. They enable people with no technical computer background to access information stored in the computer.

Magnetic Ink, Optical Character, and Bar Code Readers (I). Checks usually have numbers in magnetic ink printed at the bottom, allowing them to be read by a computer. Numbers printed in magnetic ink can be detected and interpreted by a *magnetic ink character recognition (MICR)* device. Once the character has been read, it is converted into electrical impulse (in binary form) to be used in a bank's computer to debit and credit the appropriate accounts. *Optical character readers (OCRs)* use pattern recognition, or the ability to recognize a symbol as a familiar form. Some insurers print information on the return stub of the billing notice so that it can be processed by an optical character reader to eliminate the manual data entry of the payment information. The most familiar bar code is the universal product code used in grocery and other stores to reduce checkout time and to keep accurate and timely inventory records. Some insurance companies use laser printers to print the entire policy document. In addition, they also print special bar codes on the documents identifying who is receiving the material (for example, the mortgagee or the insured). These codes are then used as input by computerized output mailing systems to determine the correct stuffers to insert into the envelopes along with the policy documents.

Printing Devices (O). Printing output is the most common form of computer output. Computer printers differ in the means employed to produce the image on paper. Some use fonts similar to that on an electric typewriter to print a single character at a time while others use laser and electrophotographic technology to print an entire page at a time. Various printing devices are in use today and many more are being developed. Further development is sorely needed. Since printing is still mechanical rather than purely electronic (as are the internal operations of the CPU), it is the slowest part of the computer system. Many computer systems are held back in their processing because of the amount of printed output required. *Spooling* (sending print images to a disk or a memory buffer) offers some relief from the bottleneck of lower speed printer operations. Even so, the insurance industry is particularly affected by this limitation of computer systems because of the industry's heavy printed output requirements.

Computer Output Microfilm (O). A computer output micro-filmer is a device that combines electronic, photo-optical, and electro-mechanical techniques for the purpose of converting digitized computer output into human-readable images and automatically recording these images on microfilm or microfiche. The acronym *COM* is often applied to such film. Some users flinch at the thought of replacing paper with film. There are factors offsetting these anxieties. A film cassette occupies less than 1 percent of the space required for a stack of equivalent paper reports, and a sheet of microfiche occupies less than 0.05 percent as much space as equivalent paper. Similar proportions hold for weight. Since COM media have indexes to the material contained on them, data can usually be retrieved in far less time than is required to access a paper document.

Special I/O Devices. Some devices do not fit easily into the established categories. An example is the automatic airline ticket vendor now found in some airports. The vendor is designed to accept credit cards, retrieve flight information, and issue a ticket on the spot. Another example is the automatic teller machine now found at banks and other financial institutions. These machines collect deposits, dispense cash, and perform other banking functions. As these special purpose units demonstrate, input/output devices can take on various characteristics and can be designed to fill almost any special need.

Supporting Devices [10]

Since the central processing unit is the "center" of the computer, all other devices are sometimes called *peripherals*. In addition to input/output devices, peripherals include devices used to support either the CPU or the I/O devices. Most of these machines are used for secondary memory or nonvolatile permanent storage because they provide for storage accessible to the CPU but not actually resident in the CPU.

Secondary Storage.

Magnetic Tape. Magnetic tapes (often called "mag tapes") are long, narrow ribbons typically mounted on reels. The standard size contains 2,400 feet of tape on a reel about ten inches in diameter. Tape cartridge systems read and write on magnetic tape contained in a four-by-five-by-one-inch cartridge. A tape cartridge can hold the same amount of data as a tape reel. As the name indicates, portions of the tape are magnetized so that data may be stored and read. The process works in a way similar to audio tape recorders. *Tape drives* read and write magnetic tape. The major advantages of magnetic tape are its relatively low cost and its large storage capacity. The primary disadvantage of magnetic tape is that it provides sequential access only. For example, if the information desired is located on the end of the reel, it is necessary to pass the entire reel of tape before the desired section can be read, obviously a very time-consuming procedure. Nevertheless, magnetic tape is one of the most common forms of auxiliary memory (storage) used today.

Cassette Tape. Cassette tape is used on some small computers, especially personal computers, because of its convenience and its similarity to standard magnetic tape. Its sequential nature makes it suitable as a disk drive backup storage and recovery medium for mini and personal computers.

Disks. Although disk storage is more expensive per bit of data than magnetic tape, it is better suited for finding the specific information sought from a given file quickly. Disks are called *direct access* or *random access devices.*

Disk drives, the machines that transfer data to and from a disk, are found on most computers operating today. Disk drives vary in their size, portability, and capacity for data. Disks resemble phonograph records, though they have no grooves. They contain a coating of iron oxide and are written on and read in a way similar to magnetic tapes. The data is read by a mechanism that hovers slightly above the disk platter (at a height less than the thickness of a human hair) and detects magnetic signals.

The popularity of disk storage has increased rapidly in recent years as the popularity of terminals and personal computers has created the need for large amounts of data to be immediately available, that is, *online.* Magnetic tape is, of course, unsuitable for this purpose since it is not designed for direct access. "Diskette" and "floppy disk" are names for inexpensive 3 1/2" and 5 1/4" versions used on personal computers. Hard disks are made of metal. Because of their rigid construction, they can be manufactured with higher storage densities and permit faster access than floppy disks.

Others. Other devices provide storage for high volumes of data. *Disk packs* contain several hard disks in a single case. *Optical laser disks* are similar to the compact disks used in stereo music systems. One type is called CD-ROM, for compact disk, read-only memory. COM refers to computer output microform, or computer output direct to microfiche or microfilm.

Other Supporting Devices. Computer rooms frequently contain more equipment than has been described here. The other machines in

Exhibit 1-1
Computer System

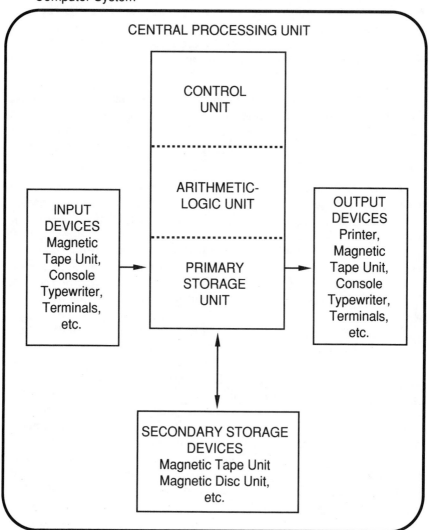

a computer system control the devices discussed. These are necessary because of the way the computer operates (a "simple-minded" machine working very, very fast). These include *channels* and *control units*. It is not important to know the names of these machines, only that they exist and are there to support the equipment which has been discussed. Exhibit 1-1 depicts the major hardware components in a typical computer system.

COMPUTER SOFTWARE

Software is the term for the programs that run the computer. Software is now produced and offered for sale by an enormous number of organizations. An insurance company has the opportunity to purchase a payroll system or a complete personal or commercial policy processing system, rather than employ its own staff to produce these programs. Agents are faced with a bewildering array of software packages and systems to automate the tasks of the agency. Almost every shopping center in the country has a store selling general purpose software. This standard software, particularly spreadsheet and word processing software, has found many applications on the personal computers used by insurance people at home and in the office.

Types of Computer Languages [11]

Machine Languages. The first computers ran on instructions expressed in machine language. Machine language means the "electrical" binary language of *on* and *off* commands that the computer understands. It is the *only* language that the computer understands. Any other language must go through a sort of "translation" into machine language before the computer can understand it.

Since the computer can deal only with information in binary form, machine language, necessarily, must be binary. It is, and, in fact, looks just like a string of binary numbers. A specific program instruction in machine language might look something like this:

$$110011101100110111001010001111101$$

This looks like a random string of binary digits. To the central processing unit of a computer, however, it could have a very specific meaning. It is the bit pattern that tells the computer what to do.

The first part of the instruction tells the computer what the function to be performed is (ADD, SUBTRACT, and so on) and is called the *op code*, or *operation code*. The layout of the rest of the instruction is determined by the op code, but usually includes the data to be used in performing the function or address of the data to be used in performing the function. The first computer programmers had to be quite precise in writing instructions for the computer. The work was tedious and errors were almost impossible to detect until the computer executed the instructions. Understandably, the personal computer revolution would not have occurred had this remained the only way a non-DP professional could communicate with a computer.

Symbolic Language. The disadvantages associated with machine language led to the development of symbolic language, the second generation of computer languages, in the early 1950s. Someone realized that if "01001" meant "subtract" to the computer, a symbol, such as "S," might be substituted for "01001" and the computer could internally convert the "S" to "01001." Soon, each of the computer's instructions had some mnemonic code (for example, ZA for Zero and Add). This was so much of an improvement that symbolic addresses were developed. Symbolic addresses allow the programmer to give a name, such as ANSWER, to a certain address in storage where the answer to a problem was stored. At the beginning of the program the programmer would specify that ANSWER referred to a certain address. After that, whenever the programmer wanted to refer to that address, he or she simply used the word ANSWER rather than the numerical designation of the address. This saved a great deal of time and, of course, was much easier to remember. Other improvements that were later added to this type of language freed the programmer from having to give the exact address for each instruction. The programmer now had only to specify the address of the first instruction. All other instructions would be stored according to sequence by the processor. This became a tremendous help whenever it was necessary to modify a program. In machine language, the insertion of a new instruction required the renumbering of the addresses of all the subsequent instructions in the program. With symbolic language, that renumbering could be handled much more easily. With all these mnemonics, computer programs began to resemble the English language to a very limited degree. For example, the following statement instructs the computer to retrieve a record from the file associated with PAYFILE and store it in memory starting at the address defined for PAYREC.

GET   PAYFILE, PAYREC

This form of communication still involves a one-to-one relationship between the number of instructions in the symbolic language program and the machine language program. That is, every instruction that the programmer writes in symbolic language must be converted into a specific machine language instruction.

Symbolic language is used when efficient use of the machine is the highest priority because it is machine rather than problem-oriented. Many personal computer and video arcade games are programmed in

The insurance agent needs to know the whereabouts of the source code for the programs his or her computer uses! This statement needs some explanation. Many insurance agencies have an in-house computer system. These systems rarely use software created within the insurance agencies. Instead, the software packages are purchased from and maintained by vendors. For their own protection, the vendors cannot release source programs. Like the secret formula for a soft drink the source program, carefully guarded, is the essence of what the vendor has to sell to the agent. But what would happen if the vendor got out of the insurance agency software market? This might happen because the vendor lost its expertise, went out of business, or simply lost interest in the insurance agency market. If the vendor quit, the agent would be left with the agency records in a computer system whose design could not be upgraded or modified. Obviously, then, the agent should not purchase a software system unless the system vendor offers some protection in terms of ultimate access to the source program. The solution is an ingenious one: The source code is placed in escrow and becomes available to the user if the vendor fails to perform as specified in the contract. An insurance company (or any other software buyer) should have the same protective feature provided by the software purchase agreement.

symbolic language because of the fast response times desired. Each CPU chip has its own symbolic and machine language, thus giving the programmer flexibility in taking advantage of the design of the machine. However, programs written in symbolic language for one type of computer will not run on another.

The software aid that translates the symbolic language program into the machine language program is called the *assembler*. The program as written by the programmer is called the *source program*. After it is translated by the assembly program, it is referred to as the *object program*. A computer cannot process a source program, only an object program.

Procedure-Oriented Languages. *Procedural languages,* the third generation, came into use in the 1960s. As their name suggests, these third generation languages, also known as *high-level languages* (FORTRAN, COBOL, PL/1, BASIC, Pascal) are considered to be procedure-oriented or procedural languages. Procedure-oriented languages are generally "portable" (can be used on more than one computer); symbolic languages, as noted above, are not. This difference became very important when companies replaced early computers with newer, larger computers and found that new programs were needed to replace the old ones. Procedure-oriented languages are designed to be run on many different computers. These programs must be translated into machine language by a software aid called a *compiler*. As mentioned earlier, the program as written by the programmer is referred to as a source program. After it is compiled, an object program is produced. The compiler and assembler can be thought of as two slightly different translators that convert programs to machine readable form. Exhibit 1-2 depicts the language translation process.

Although symbolic language is still used for many purposes, procedure-oriented languages dominate. Procedure-oriented languages are used when programmer efficiency rather than machine or computer efficiency has the highest priority.

While certainly not covering all the procedural languages currently in use within the insurance industry, the following section will touch on most of them. All of them are procedure-oriented languages. No one language is consistently preferable to another. Each has its own advantages, disadvantages, and characteristics.[12]

COBOL. The most commonly used language in the business world today is COBOL (COmmon Business Oriented Language). COBOL was first published in 1960. The development of this language was actually a project carried out by a committee. The express purpose of this group, the CODASYL (COnference of DAta SYstems Languages), was to produce a language that would both serve the business community and help users achieve program compatibility (portability from one computer to another). Most computer manufacturers provide COBOL compilers for their machines. As with human languages, there are "dialects" of COBOL. One of the most noticeable features of a COBOL program is that it looks something like English. There are, of course, COBOL versions in French, Spanish, and other languages.

One of the prime advantages of COBOL is the flexibility it allows programmers in formatting the source code. Unfortunately, this flexibility is also one of its prime disadvantages—the language itself requires no conformity in structure. Flexibility in a language is no liability to the person who writes the program. However, the person who must later revise or modify that program will have a very difficult time. Leaders in the industry have addressed this problem with *structured programming* techniques. These techniques impose a logic which programmers are encouraged to follow.

Exhibit 1-2
Language Translation Process

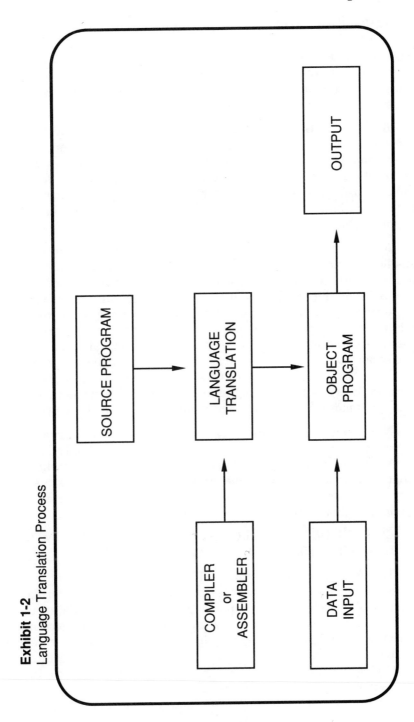

FORTRAN. FORTRAN (FORmula TRANslation) was developed in the 1950s as a scientific-mathematic language. FORTRAN enables engineers and scientists to program the computer in familiar symbols, very similar to the language of mathematics. FORTRAN caught on quickly and remains a standard language even though its use in the business world has been limited.

BASIC. BASIC (Beginner's All-purpose Symbolic Instruction Code) was developed as an easy to learn language suitable for teaching programming to beginners. It soon became popular because of its simplicity and close resemblance to English. BASIC has found its greatest use on personal computers because it allows someone with little or no background to sit down at a terminal and begin writing simple problem-solving programs.

RPG. RPG (Report Program Generator) has found its niche in smaller business computer operations. As its name indicates, RPG's original purpose was to produce reports. It was not meant to be a sophisticated, highly flexible language although subsequent versions are evolving in that direction. Rather than writing a program in a relatively free form, RPG requires the programmer to use prescribed specification sheets. Input is described on one sheet, output on another, and so on. Some programmers exclude RPG as an actual programming language, insisting that the RPG compiler produces a program from specifications given it by a programmer. Nonetheless, it enjoys common usage and more than a little respect among those who have used it.

Nonprocedural Languages.[13] A nonprocedural language tells the computer *what* is to be accomplished rather than exactly *how* to do it. A compiler or interpreter determines *how* the computer should do what is asked for. For example, an agency's personal lines customer service representative might sit down at a terminal connected to the agency's computer and type:

LIST ALL OF MY HOMEOWNERS POLICIES WITH LIMITS LESS THAN 300,000.

This is a complete "program." It leaves the decisions as to what subset of homeowners policies to select, how the list should be formatted, when to skip pages, how to number pages, how to sort the insured's name and/or policy number, and what limits to use to the software. If the software makes the wrong decisions or assumptions, the statement can be made as specific as necessary to obtain the desired results.

Giving instructions to a taxi driver will illustrate the distinction between procedural and nonprocedural languages. With a procedural language you have to tell the driver exactly *how* to proceed: "Drive 500 yards. Turn left. Drive 380 yards. Turn right. Drive to the traffic light. If the light is green...." With a nonprocedural language, tell the taxi driver *what* you want: "Take me to the movie theater on Malvern Street."

Fourth-Generation Languages.[14] Fourth-generation languages, such as INTELLECT and FOCUS were created for two main reasons, first so that nonprogrammers could obtain the information they need from computers, and second to speed up the programming process. Some fourth-generation languages are nonprocedural. Some are procedural, but results can be obtained with far fewer instructions or lines of programming code than with COBOL. Many contain both procedural and nonprocedural statements or instructions. A fourth-generation language should allow a nonprofessional programmer to obtain results after learning a portion of the language in not more than a two-day training class, make intelligent assumptions about what the user wants, and be designed for on-line interactive operation.

Fourth-generation languages cannot satisfy the needs of all computer applications. They are not general purpose but are more limited in application. However, these languages enable users to obtain the results they need fast, whereas traditional programming in COBOL does not.

Types of Software

We have discussed the various types of computer programming languages and where they are utilized in the application development process. The software "pie" can be sliced in a different way—into system software and applications software. In general, *systems software*, is primarily concerned with the operation of the computer. *Applications software* is primarily concerned with solving problems.

Systems Software. Systems software includes the *operating system*—the group of programs that operate the computer. The operating system controls the use of other programs.

Program libraries are stored on a secondary storage device, usually a disk, and are called upon when needed. For example, an insurance company's software library may contain a program that produces a report of written premiums classified by the insurance agency that produced the business. The original program was probably written by a programmer sitting at a CRT or personal computer. Once debugged and tested, the program is stored in the computer's program library. Whenever the program is to be run, the user or programmer needs to insert the proper program disk (if the program is not stored on hard disk), type a few characters on the CRT or personal computer monitor to retrieve the program, and start running it.

Language Translators. This type of systems software includes assemblers and compilers. They translate symbolic and procedure-oriented language into machine language. Another common type of systems software used with interactive terminals is the *teleprocessing monitor*. This type of software operates under control of the operating system and acts as a mini-operating system for those programs being utilized by interactive terminals. The very nature of processing with interactive terminals requires some additional systems software to remove details from application programs.

Database Management Systems. By enabling the user to define, create, access, manipulate, and output the information stored in a database, these systems add an additional file access method to those available through the computer's operating system. Because of this, database management systems are classified as systems software.

Database technology allows an organization's data to be processed as an integrated whole rather than as a collection of tape files and sequential and random disk data sets. A database management system (DBMS) is the interface between application programs designed to use them and the organization's databases. A database management system performs three major functions:

1. It translates the application's request for data to determine the desired database operations. These requests may be expressed in terms of logical data relationships, such as "retrieve the names of all policyholders in territory six."
2. Requests specified in this manner are then transformed into operations to be performed on the database files such as "retrieve record 5050 from disk 58 and record 79 for disk 27," and so on.
3. Finally, data is transferred from secondary storage to main memory for processing by the application.

Utility Programs. Utility programs that perform very specific functions are also considered as systems software. These programs sort, merge, copy, or move data from one device to another, recover inadvertently deleted files, erase, rename, and perform other operations on files.

Applications Software. Applications programs give the computer instructions for performing specific tasks. While systems software tells the computer *how* to compute, applications software tells the computer *what* to compute—that is, how to perform the specific input, calculation, control, and output operations necessary for a particular task. Neither is more important than the other, for they operate in mutual dependence. Applications software exists to perform information processing tasks and produce output while systems software is necessary to enable a computer to run applications programs. In general, applications software uses procedure-oriented languages.

Within an insurance company, applications software may include the policy processing, claims, legal, personnel and payroll, property inventory, and many other systems. Within an insurance agency, operating software may include the agency management system, rating programs, and word processing programs. A risk manager's systems software is likely to include special risk management programs as well as word processing and other less task-specific software.

The popularity of personal computers is due in large part to the application software available for them. The PC owner has access to thousands of application programs to meet practically any imaginable need. Much of this software is readily available by mail order or from neighborhood computer stores. Some of it is free (freeware) and some (shareware) is distributed free with a request that the user pay a small fee after deciding to use it. The best known software is likely to be priced between $75 and $500 and have copyright protection. The market for applications software is highly competitive, and purchasers are price-conscious. Innovative software is likely to be followed in the market-place by clone versions that are usually less expensive but not necessarily less capable.

The varieties of applications software seem endless. One can buy software for keeping a calendar, managing financial affairs, planning menus, learning a language, or completing income tax forms. Hobbyists are likely to find special software to support their particular interests. Software games are popular diversions and are often used to gain familiarity with the computer keyboard.

Popular Applications Software Packages. Three kinds of applications software should be cited as being of extraordinary value and importance. They are available for large systems and are, deservedly, the best sellers of the personal computer software world. They are the hammer, pliers, and screwdriver of the software domain. A homeowner may have dozens of tools and yet find that the majority of repairs and projects need only a hammer, pliers, and screwdriver. These three basic software tools are word processing, spreadsheet, and data management. They are available separately and as components of integrated packages.

Word Processing. Word processing software is used in the preparation of written copy, including letters, memos, documents, lists, instructions, and articles. Almost any job that can be done on a typewriter is suitable for word processing. (The notable exceptions are filling in forms and typing single envelopes.)

The advantages of word processing over using a typewriter are many. Words, paragraphs, and large blocks of text can be moved quickly and with ease. A list of addresses can be combined with text copy to produce a series of individual letters to the persons on the list. Word processing software often includes a feature that checks the spelling of common words. It may allow the computer to search for a word or phrase and find it each time it appears in a document. With these and other features, word processing packages bring convenience and efficiency to the recording—and changing—of words.

Spreadsheet. Spreadsheet software is used for the preparation and presentation of numerical data. The format used, itself called a spreadsheet, is simply a matrix or table of rows and columns. Each cell, or intersection of a column and row, can contain figures or letters. Headings and labels can be placed where needed.

One uses a spreadsheet by creating a model (called a template) of the desired table. Into this model are placed the mathematical formulas that perform the desired calculations. For example, the user can give the instruction that the figure in column E (auto expense) is the figure in column D (miles) multiplied by $.265 (mileage rate) and that this formula is to be used in cells E6 through E30. Each time a figure is entered in any of the cells in Column D in the range D6 through D30, the computer instantly multiplies that figure by $.265 and enters the result in the adjacent cell in Column E. This simple multiplication illustration barely hints at the ability of spreadsheet software to use complex mathematical formulas. In addition to cell calculation instructions, the template usually contains instructions for the calculation of whatever column and row totals are desired and instructions for labels and headings.

The enormous popularity of spreadsheet software stems from the ease and speed with which calculations—and recalculations—are made. In the example given above, suppose the mileage rate of $.265 is raised to $.28. Only a few keystrokes are needed for the user to change the instruction. The computer then automatically revises the entries in cells E6 through E30 and the column and row totals that are affected. This power is often used in "what if" analysis. The user can ask how auto expenses and total expenses would be affected if the mileage rate were changed, or if mileage were reduced by 10 percent or by 12 percent. The computer provides, in a matter of seconds, the information wanted even if the spreadsheet is a large one with, say, 32 columns and 94 rows.

Spreadsheet packages typically include graphics software. This allows the presentation of spreadsheet data in such forms as bar charts, pie charts, and line graphs. The graphics produced are often of such high quality that they can be reproduced in printed documents or made into slides for presentations.

Data Management. The third major type of popular software goes by a variety of names: data management, file management, and database management. The purposes of this software are to provide for the efficient storage and rapid retrieval of large amounts of information. These purposes also apply to the *database management systems* described above as a type of systems software. Unfortunately, terminology is loose and it is not easy to tell if "database management" is being used to refer to software for a giant mainframe computer or to a far more modest program purchased for use on a PC. The essential point is that the data management software that provides for the storage and retreival of information in an efficient and flexible way has earned a place among the "big three" of popular software. While it may be classified as system software in large computer systems, it is likely to be purchased in disk form as application software for use in office and home PCs.

The operation of popular data management software can be shown by an illustration. Suppose that a collector of compact discs wants to maintain an inventory of the music in his or her collection. Using data management software, the collector defines the exact format and sequence in which the desired information elements are to be entered. The following elements might be chosen: composer, title, conductor, soloists, solo instruments, and label. File management software allows the collector to extract data by any of the defined elements. The collector can instruct the computer to provide listings of all performances of the works of a given composer, of all performances of a given title, or of all recordings of a particular title that contain a piano solo. Obviously these are but three of the many retrieval possibilities. The flexibility of information retrieval is clearly the paramount advantage of data management software.

Integrated Packages. The features of the three popular software packages (word processing, spreadsheet, and data management) may be combined into an integrated package. The advantage of integration comes at a price: an integrated package is not likely to have all of the features provided by separate word processing, spreadsheet, and data management software. The primary advantage is the ability to enter data once and move it among functions—for example, to move data from the data management function into spreadsheet and graphics functions.

DATA COMMUNICATIONS

When computers were first introduced, all data processing activities were handled in a central location. The CPU, primary storage, and I/O devices were all located together. Rather than being limited to the home office, terminals are now commonplace throughout an insurer's organization. Data communications technology interconnects insurance company CPUs, terminals, personal computers, printers, and other I/O devices no matter where they are located.

Carriers and Carrier Technology [15, 16]

Data communications require a sender, a link, and a receiver. The link is provided by a carrier. A *carrier* is any system used to carry data from one location to another. Carriers include wire cables, coaxial cables, microwave and high frequency radio transmissions, communication satellites, and fiber optic cables. The capacity of a carrier is typically measured in bits of information transmitted in one second. One baud is about one bit per second. If a carrier has a capacity of 300 baud, it can transmit about 300 bits of information per second. Data can be transmitted in one of three ways—*simplex, half duplex,* and *full duplex*. With simplex, the data can flow only in one direction, like the radio in your car. Data in half duplex transmissions flows in both directions, but it can flow only in one direction at a time. Data in full duplex transmission can flow in both directions at one time. Insurance companies frequently use specially conditioned leased lines to connect the terminals in their field offices and other remote locations such as insurance agencies to their CPUs. These are telephone lines with a guaranteed level of quality wired directly between two points, bypassing the telephone company switching centers and not shared with other telephone company customers.

Providers

The organizations that supply data communication services are called data communication carriers. These companies provide the telephone lines and other communications media used to transmit data and information from one location to another. Providers are classified as either common carriers or special purpose carriers. American Telephone and Telegraph (AT&T) and General Telephone and Electronics (GTE) are two examples of common carriers. Special purpose carriers provide specialized service in the data communications industry. The IBM Information Network (IBM/IN) is an example of a special purpose carrier. IBM/IN provides a number of services for the insurance industry, including support for the IVANS network. It is available through local telephone access in many metropolitan areas in the United States. In addition to the agency/company interface related services that will be discussed in Chapter 3, IBM/IN also provides users with access to stock market information and other noninsurance information services as well.

Communication Devices

To communicate data over telephone lines and other carriers, a device is required to translate the computer's digital representation of data into an analog signal that can be transmitted over the carrier. The electronic device that transforms the sending end's data is called a *modulator*. The device at the receiving end that decodes the analog signal is known as a *demodulator*. Since two-way communication requires a modulator and demodulator at each end, these two functions are built into a single device called a modulator/demodulator or *modem*. In addition to sending data across telephone lines, modems can automatically dial and answer incoming calls under control of the software programs using them. Many PC users have equipped their computers with modems to gain access to computer information services or to exchange data with other computers.

Because telephone lines are expensive, devices have been developed that can take signals from several terminals and communicate them over one line. These devices can be divided into three general groups: multiplexers, concentrators, and special communication processors. A *multiplexer* accepts input from a collection of lines in some fixed, predetermined sequence, and outputs that data onto a single output line in the same sequence. In other words, each output time slot is dedicated to a specific input line. The disadvantage of multiplexers is that when a terminal does not have any activity, an output time slot is wasted. The output time slots are filled in strict rotation so that the receiving end can keep track of which data came from which terminal by its position in the output stream. *Concentrators* also combine input from multiple terminals for transmission down one output line. They accomplish this by using microprocessors to reduce the number of input signals to form a smaller number of output signals. Concentrators are useful where terminals have activity only a small portion of the time or where data communication costs are high. *Special communication processors* handle communications to and from CPUs. The CPU is then able to process more work without having to slow down to input from and output to its terminals and other I/O devices.

Computer Networks

The merging of computer and communication technology has replaced the concept of a single computer serving all of an organization's computing needs with that of two or more separate but interconnected computers distributing the power of automation to more and more of an organization's employees. Networks make all programs, data, and other resources available to anyone on the network without regard to the physical location of the computer or the user. Networks also permit organizations to temporarily accommodate users on another computer when their primary computer has a hardware failure.

The *local area network (LAN)* is a special type of network that connects computers and supporting devices in the same geographical location rather than multiple computers in remote locations. The LAN can be thought of as a high-speed data pipeline or electric highway connecting two or more computers, enabling them to share programs and peripheral hardware.

One advantage of a LAN is that everyone on the network has access to the most recent data. The simpler, cheaper alternative to the LAN for data exchange is to make several copies of a file on floppy disks and give each user a copy. There are drawbacks to this simple solution. Many data files are too large to fit on one or two floppy disks. When floppy disks are used, users must be careful to recycle or discard out-of-date diskettes to prevent the inadvertent use of stale information. CPU costs have dropped significantly, but the cost of essential equipment such as storage devices and high-speed line or laser printers remains high. Through the LAN, the high storage capacity of a hard-disk is available to all stations on the network. This network provides everyone with much faster access to the same data than would be possible with floppy disks. In addition to sharing hard-disk storage, the LAN allows sharing expensive computer peripherals such as color plotters, laser printers, and connections between the local area network and mainframe computers.

EVOLUTION OF COMPUTER TECHNOLOGY [17]

Today, computers can process information and solve problems thousands of times faster than the early electronic computers of the 1940s and 1950s. The development of computer technology, from electrome-chanical punched card machines and vacuum tube calculators to power-ful computers that measure speed in billionths of a second, is usually expressed in terms of generations. Unlike human generations, where it is fairly easy to distinguish one generation from another (father and son are always two different people), computer generations have somewhat arbitrary lines of demarcation. One reason for these varying views is that computer manufacturers gain an obvious marketing advantage through announcing the birth of a new generation of hardware.

Electromechanical Devices

Constructed of wire, wheels, and levers, electromechanical ma-chines that punched, tabulated, and sorted cards were the heart of information processing technology through the end of World War II. Data was stored on cards by means of holes punched in columns on the card. Originally developed by Herman Hollerith for the 1890 U.S. Census, punched card machines were later put to use by government, railroads, and insurance companies. Many punched card installations continued in operation until the functions they performed were replaced by or converted to computers in the 1960s.

The First Generation (1951-1958)

The first electronic computers were built using vacuum tubes and were noted for their bulkiness and noise. Vacuum-tube technology permitted these machines to perform calculations several times faster than tabulating machines. Some of the first computers incorporated the stored program concept that greatly expanded these early computers' ability to do complex work at high speed. Originally designed for scientific problem solving, the vacuum tube computers were eventually used for billing, payroll, accounts receivable, inventory control, and other commercial applications offering high cost savings.

The Second Generation (1958-1964)

Though the transistor was invented in 1948, it took ten years for the transistor to be perfected for use in commercial computers. When transistors replaced vacuum tubes in computers, the change was so significant that it made sense to refer to a second generation of comput-ers. The tiny transistor shortened the time needed for electrical pulses to complete a circuit. Transistors also generated much less heat, were much more reliable, and lowered production costs. Magnetic core was used for main memory. Magnetic tape and disk storage began replacing punched cards as auxiliary storage devices, while high-level languages like FORTRAN and COBOL were developed for scientific and business uses respectively.

The Third Generation (1964-1971)

The third generation of computers was distinguished by the use of integrated circuits which, because of their smaller size, allowed faster processing and greater storage capacity in the same physical area. Advances in data communications and the development of computer terminals in significant quantity and quality enabled computer users to develop online applications. Computer programming also assumed greater importance as attention focused on the development of software designed to make the most efficient and productive use of the computer.

The Fourth Generation (1971– ?)

Although there is a fair amount of agreement about when the first and second generation ended, opinions differ with respect to the end of the third generation. For many, several developments mark the beginning of the fourth generation. Very dense, large-scale integration (LSI) of both memory and logic technology is the first development. This technological development brought major gains in computer speed, capacity, and reliability. New storage devices and concepts greatly increased the amount of data that could be stored as well as the ease of handling it, permitting users with complex applications to work with millions or billions of characters of information. Last, development of the microprocessor made personal computers possible.

The Fifth Generation (?)

The second, third, and fourth generations of computer technology were each an extension of the previous generation, implemented with dramatically better technology. Fifth generation computing, as defined by the Japanese when they began their own efforts under that title in 1981, is to employ so-called *artificial intelligence* techniques on new computers utilizing very large-scale integration (VLSI) with the intent of making computers easier to use and able to mimic several characteristics of human intelligence. The hope is to make machines that can speak and understand verbal communications, make inferences, and generally deal with "knowledge" instead of raw numbers and letters.

One factor that is constant in every aspect of computer generations has been and will continue to be "more": more capacity, more speed, more options, and more complexity.

COMPUTER SYSTEMS

The terms *computer* and *computer system* are often used synonymously. The term computer system seems more appropriate, if for no other reason than the connotation of complexity. To understand anything of great complexity we tend to divide it up into pieces of more manageable size. "Divide and conquer" might be a suitable battle cry for those who wish to understand the field of computers. Computer systems can be divided three ways—by size, by response time, and by structure.

Classifying by Size [18]

At one time, the sole measurement of a company's progress in computer usage was the size of the computer itself. This is no longer true. Computers are becoming not only bigger and faster; they are also becoming smaller and faster. Sophisticated computer users can now have access to a proliferation of computer equipment, including multiple computers of various sizes, from pocket calculators to mammoth systems occupying a floor or more of huge buildings.

The important development is that every computer customer or potential customer can choose from a broad range of computers, differing in design and operation as much as in size. As this trend continues, classification of computers by size should become more difficult, while the chances of a company finding the computer of "just the right size" should increase.

Microcomputers. Microcomputers can be best defined as single-user computers with an average system cost of $12,000 or less that sit on top of a desk or workstation. Since microcomputers are also referred to as personal computers (PCs), the two terms will be used interchangeably throughout this book.

The development of the silicon chip in 1971 made the first microcomputer possible. The chip was originally designed to be the "brain" in small, handheld electronic calculators, but it has since been adapted to many other uses. The heart of the microcomputer is the microprocessor—a miniature central processing unit complete with arithmetic/logic unit, input/output control logic, and registers for storing data. The technology of microcomputer design offers staggering possibilities.

Personal computers are a common sight in insurance companies and agencies. Insurance industry employees from company executives to clerical workers use microcomputers for preparation of reports and budgets, chart and graphics generation, project management, word processing, desktop publishing, personal and commercial lines rating, underwriting and claim management, financial modeling, statistical analysis, and other previously time-consuming manual tasks. Personal computers also provide basic agency automation support of client and policy information as well as the agency's marketing programs.

Microcomputer proliferation within the insurance industry is a result of the many benefits they offer. Personal computers are increasing employee productivity and enriching the jobs of both clerical and professional employees. By simplifying budgeting and other analytical tasks, PCs permit the assignment of these tasks to secretaries and administrative assistants, allowing managers to use their own time in other tasks. Personal computers are also more cost effective than terminals connected to the mini and mainframe computers they often replace. The word processing, mass storage, and data processing capabilities of micros simply do not exist in the typical terminal. Microcomputers are also being used for local data entry and error checking. When used for these tasks, data can be collected and stored for data transmission to company mainframe computers from agency and company offices at predetermined intervals or on demand. Local processing reduces the processing load on company mainframe computers, lengthening the intervals between mainframe upgrades. Microcomputer based local processing also avoids the down time and slow response problems periodically experienced by users of mini and mainframe computers. Finally, PCs allow managers to perform complex analyses, answer "what if" questions, and provide a range of decision support functions.

Minicomputers. Minicomputers are multi-user computers requiring their own floor space for CPU, computer memory, disk drives, and printers. Digital Equipment Corporation produced the first commercial minicomputer in 1965. Originally considered a fad, or at most, an extremely small segment of the market, minicomputers have become a mainstay of the industry.

Minicomputers offer the following advantages.

Adaptability. Minicomputers, like the large-scale or mainframe machines, are also adaptable. The large number of peripheral devices

The Hidden Costs of Personal Computers [19]

In many companies, the investment in personal computers and peripheral equipment is not understood as well as it should be. While managers know about the proliferation of personal computers in the company, many do not know the full range of costs associated with PCs. The table below breaks out the direct and hidden costs associated with upgrading a personal computer from an independent desktop machine to a workstation with connections to other machines.

Direct costs
Personal computer
Hard disk
Software
Printer

Hidden costs
Hardware for a local area network connection
Large peripheral devices (such as large disk storage and laser printers)
Local area network software and multi-user application software
Mainframe access charges
Other costs (such as support personnel)

The issue, however, is not how to clamp down in a reactionary manner, but how to manage the costs so that the enormous business potential inherent in personal computers is realized productively and efficiently.

available to minicomputer purchasers today offer them the ability to "mix and match." The average system cost of a typical minicomputer system ranges from $12,000 to $700,000, depending on the number of devices (input/output, auxiliary storage, and so on) used.

Relative Low Cost. Compared with large-scale or mainframe computers—especially those which existed when minicomputers were introduced—cost of "minis" made computers accessible to many more people. When new, minis actually enlarged the computer industry by making computers available to smaller users, especially insurance agencies, which previously were prohibited from taking advantage of automation because of the cost involved.

Ease of Use. The third generation started the use of sophisticated operating systems. Although this software offered many benefits to large computer users, it also tended to add a great deal of overhead. This overhead often led to inefficiency in the operation of the computer. Large data processing departments evolved where only a few programmers had been needed before. This put more and more people between the computer and those who originally wanted the computer. The minicomputer cut through all this bureaucracy by taking a small version of the computer and putting it with the people who needed it.

Communications. Minicomputers can function not only as computers, but also as terminals. Data communications technology developed to allow minicomputers and large-scale computers to "communicate" with each other in a network. This feature enabled the minicomputer to cope with one of its disadvantages—limited storage capacity. To access large data files, the minicomputer could be "hooked up" to a large-scale computer (referred to as the host computer).

Size and Durability. Large-scale computers were notorious for their tremendous weight and for their space requirements. Paradoxically, they had to be handled with kid gloves because of their sensitivity to temperature and humidity conditions. Minicomputers were smaller and more rugged. They could be located where the work was performed. Ironically, this happened at the time when many organizations built elaborate showcases in which to house their computers. Moreover, minicomputers, because they were smaller, did not produce the tremendous heat of the larger machines (which is of more than minor importance for people who must work in the same room with one).

There are also disadvantages to minicomputers:

Simplistic. Many jobs are too complex or too large to be handled by minicomputers.

Limited Storage. Storage size is, of course, much less for a minicomputer than for a large-scale computer.

Slower Execution. Instructions are generally executed at a slower speed in minicomputers as compared to mainframes. This is not as much of a disadvantage as may first appear, however, since there is not as much going on internally (operating system software) as in the larger machines. Besides, a user's main concern should be the overall through-put of the machine (how much total work is accomplished in a given time) and not the number of nanoseconds it takes for one instruction to be executed.

Less Powerful Capabilities Overall. The net result of these disadvantages is that a minicomputer is less powerful than a large-scale or mainframe computer. Minicomputers are being designed with more storage capacity and faster execution speeds—some are comparable to large-scale systems in these respects. But, practically speaking, these cease to be minicomputers, as that term is generally understood. With the rapid development of microcomputers and the proliferation of computers of all sizes, the term "minicomputer" may well become an anachronism in the future. If so, it will certainly be remembered as one of the most popular "buzzwords" of the 1970s and 1980s.

Large-Scale or Mainframe Computers. Mainframe computers are so large that they require a separate room for the computer itself and the memory, disk and tape drives, printers, and environmental systems necessary to support them. These include the IBM 370 line. The 360 series also fits into this category, although technological advances and attendant price reductions per unit of computer power make the 360 appear feeble compared to newer equipment in this class.

The IBM 303X, 308X, 309X series of computers are probably the most popular computers in the insurance industry today. Available in various sizes and models, they fill the needs of both very large and fairly small insurance firms. More major mainframe product announcements by IBM and other manufacturers are expected to occur almost routinely in the years ahead.

The characteristics of large-scale computers include the following.

Heavy Support. With the average system cost of $700,000 or more, purchases of computers of this size provide computer manufacturers with the incentive and funds to offer a wide range of supporting services. These include, but are definitely not limited to, full-time specialists to assist in the most technical aspects of computer operation, software consulting, long-range planning assistance, seminars, advance education, and meetings with other users.

High Speed Printers. Printers that produce 2,000 lines of print per minute are not uncommon with large-scale computer systems. Printers using laser and electrophotographic technology can print up to 120 lines per page and 167 to 526 pages, or over 210,000 lines per minute.

Large Disk Storage. These systems are noted for their large capacity for data. The disk is the most common medium for the masses of data that are now being stored.

Communications Ability. Today's large-scale computers are designed with ease of telecommunications as a key feature. Operating systems have grown in size and complexity to such an extent that they can control a large, sophisticated network of computers and terminals.

Multiprocessing. While multiprogramming is the running of two programs concurrently, multiprocessing is running two or more processors simultaneously. The IBM 3084, for example, links four powerful computers in parallel processing. These central processing units can operate in tandem, in which case they are called "twin CPUs." The duplication of critical computer hardware results in a system capable of continuing operation while failing portions are isolated and repaired. It is also possible to have multiple processing units that differ in size and capacity.

Off-Loaded CPU. Off-loading the CPU means removing functions normally performed by the central processing unit and putting them in some supporting device. For example, a front-end controller is used to control certain aspects of the network.

For example, the CPU must maintain "constant" communication with each terminal so that when someone requests information from the terminal, the CPU can respond. To maintain "constant" communication, the CPU checks with the first terminal to see if there is a message to be sent. If not, it goes to the second terminal in the network (each terminal is assigned an address). After the CPU has checked each terminal, it starts over and checks them all again. This continuous process is called polling. The computer's speed makes it seem as if there is "constant" communication with the terminals. The need for off-loading arises because each time the CPU checks a terminal, it is executing instructions and using up valuable time. If a front-end controller is used for polling, when a terminal does request information from the CPU, the front-end controller (sometimes called front-end processor) simply "passes" the request on to the CPU. The front-end processor can be a minicomputer used to perform this function.

Classifying by Response Mode

The concepts of batch processing and online processing have already been described. This section will elaborate on each and explain how these two different modes of processing coexist in many computer installations.

Batch Processing. In the batch processing mode, data is converted into some computer readable form, gathered into batches, and then taken physically or telecommunicated periodically to the computer for processing. This "period" could be every hour, every day, or every week; most often, it is every day or overnight. Turnaround time is quite slow when compared with online processing, but for many purposes batch processing works quite well. Most important is that it makes efficient use of the computer's time; computers work most efficiently on large volumes of similar data that can be processed sequentially.

Batch processing was the most common form of processing in the second generation and during the early part of the third generation. As time went on, computer speeds and capacities increased, and data processing costs decreased relative to employee costs, managers questioned whether the efficiency of the computer was more important than the efficiency of the people using it. For example, overnight processing dictated that any error made by someone in the input data would not be detected until the computer could *edit* it. It is common practice for data entry personnel to check one another's work by rekeying the same information. This is called *verifying*. This process catches some of the errors before the data enters the computer for processing. Because errors detected by computer edits were usually not returned to the person making them until the following morning, worker efficiency was sacrificed. A data entry operator could make one mistake and, because the computer would not catch it until that night, might go on making the same mistake on subsequent work processed that day. It is psychologically better to detect errors and correct them as soon as possible.

During the early 1960s, many companies computerized such functions as inventory control, billing, and order follow-up. The computer produced monthly reports and the like in a clearly satisfactory manner, but did not provide fast access to data that was completely current. The parts warehouse with computerized inventory could have a listing of all items in stock, but it would only be as current as the last batch run. The accounts receivable report of an insurance broker was similarly out of date on most working days. The computer system was not as good as the old manual system in this respect. With batch processing, the ability to go "directly to the file" was limited.

Online Processing. It would be inaccurate to say that online processing chooses human efficiency over computer efficiency. Instead, online processing offers a more desirable balance between the two. The term *online* signifies a direct, current link with the computer. This usually implies the presence of a terminal or PC. However, it can be another device as commonplace as the telephone. Ordinary touch-tone telephones are used by customers of many banks and savings institutions as terminals. Obviously, telephones are slow and limited in flexibility when compared to terminals and PCs.

To say that one is online with the computer does not specify the functions the terminal can perform. The system design might provide a highly limited capability, such as policyholder data verification. On the other hand, remote terminals might be given full capability to retrieve, add, and change any data in a policyholder file.

Online processing is a boon to many computer users, including programmers. They can maintain their programs by using a terminal located at their desks. Other users, too, are eager to take advantage of the potential provided by online terminals. A terminal allows remote use of at least a portion of the organization's computer. It also allows rental of a terminal or microcomputer and purchase of service from a vendor's computer (timesharing).

Real-time processing is a specific type of online processing through which the user not only has direct access to the computer and its files, but can also modify or use those files immediately and directly. Real-time processing exists when information is processed in time to be used in a business transaction. A familiar example is the airline reservation computer. Space availability is checked, space committed, and the ticket issued while the customer waits at the ticket counter. As you might expect, only a portion of online processing is real-time processing.

When online processing became a practical reality for many companies in the third and fourth computer generations, did they abandon batch processing? No, because adopting the online mode did not require abandoning batch processing. Many applications are still processed most efficiently in the batch mode at night with data collected by the online systems during the day.

Hybrid Processing. Hybrid processing combines features of batch and online processing. A data entry operator may use a terminal for data input, an element of online processing. The computer holds the data on some auxiliary storage device (that is, tape or disk) until a sufficient number have accumulated, and then it processes the data, thus providing an element of batch processing. Hybrid processing is the basis of many insurance company personal and commercial policy processing and claim systems.

Classifying by Structure

At one time, a major consideration in the design of computer systems was whether they provided for centralized or distributed data processing. The evolution of computer technology, however, has made that issue far more complex.

Centralized Data Processing.[20]   Centralized data processing concentrates the processing of information in one or a few locations. A centralized automation policy seeks to distribute data processing in a manner that maintains managerial control over information.   Data processing activity and growth are kept under control by a central data processing department which uses one or more mainframe computers to service a network of terminals. Centralized data processing, because of the economies of scale it provides, can justify the purchase of expensive hardware and software.   With the centralization of data processing, management can monitor adherence to its standards for system design, quality, compatibility, and auditability, as well as keeping track of the organization's overall automation policy. Centralized data processing is oriented toward top-down control, control of computing costs, control of computing uses, and, in some cases, control over the information being processed.

Excessive centralization of data processing can result in the creation of bureaucracy that fails to meet user requirements for information. Centralized DP operations also tend to develop resistance to change and may fail to exploit new developments as a result.

Extreme centralization has technical dangers. As the network of terminals connected to the central host computers grow in size and complexity, terminal response time decreases. Another drawback is the total unavailability of terminal usage when the mainframe fails.

Distributed Data Processing (DDP).[21]   DDP distributes computer "intelligence" throughout the computer network rather than having it all at the host computer. The development of the minicomputer was one of the prime forces facilitating DDP. Minicomputers and microcomputers are located in the branch or department of the user to perform some processing functions and to communicate with the mainframe. Decentralized data processing facilitates bottom-up productivity improvement, improved exploitation of automation for departmental tasks, and the design of systems to meet user needs.

There are a number of pitfalls involved with DDP. Security may be difficult; applications that process a large mass of data with high security requirements must be processed centrally. If not carefully controlled, DDP can result in the incompatibility of data because the same data may be defined differently in each location or because the disks used in one computer cannot be used in another.   Creeping escalation of machine costs is another drawback to DDP. The first DDP application is often easy to install. As new applications are added, complexity, main memory requirements, the number of terminals, and auxiliary storage requirements increase.

Complex Structures. The centralization versus decentralization debate is not one over an either/or issue. Properly addressed, the issue can be resolved in a system design that provides the best of both worlds.

The proliferation of micros as stand-alone personal workstations, a pitfall of uncontrolled decentralization, has raised the question of how to share data among incompatible micros, minicomputers, and mainframe computers. Insurance industry employees do not work in isolation. Even though they may use personal computers, they still want to be able to retain some of the benefits provided by a centralized system including the ability to exchange messages with their co-workers and to access information from several computer files while preparing a document or analyzing data. Balancing and shifting power between an organization's management, information systems area, and users is a continuous process. Each group has an important role to play in making sure that the company has the right level of support from its information systems.

SUMMARY

This chapter presents an overview of the vast subject usually signified by the single word *computer*. What makes a computer a computer is its ability to operate under the control of an internally stored program of instructions. That program directs the accomplishment of the major functions of input, output, storage, calculation, and control.

Thinking of a computer as a mechanical or electronic device is far too narrow a view. A computer or computer system contains three major components: hardware, software, and people. Within the realm of hardware, the central processing unit is the hub of all activity. It contains the processes that make a computer a computer. It performs calculations and logical comparisons and has memory for storing of the data and instructions currently being processed. Connected to the central processing unit are input and output devices and peripheral equipment, including equipment that allows one computer to communicate with other computers.

Computer software (instruction programs) are written in languages that have become progressively easier to use. A general understanding of popular computer languages is helpful in understanding the power and problems of computer processing. However, most people employ computers not by using languages but by using prewritten or off-the-shelf application programs. The most popular of these are word processing, spreadsheet, and data management programs, and integrated packages that combine them.

Computers have had an interesting, if short, history. The early generations of computer development were marked by drastic changes in technology. Progress is now more evolutionary. In surveying the landscape of automation, it is helpful to classify computers into various categories. The lines between categories blur as new computers are developed. For example, it is difficult to place some systems into the commonly used categories of microcomputers, minicomputers, and large systems. Similarly, a given system may provide both batch and online processing modes. Further, an organization's information system may incorporate features of both centralized and distributed processing.

The terms and concepts in this chapter are primarily descriptive. They detail, among other things, what a computer is, how it works, and in what form it may be found. They provide the beginning of a basic vocabulary for dealing with a resource of ever-increasing importance in the insurance world.

Chapter Notes

1. American National Standards Institute, *American National Standard Vocabulary for Information Processing*, X3.12-170, 1970.
2. Donald H. Sanders, *Computers in Business—An Introduction*, 3rd ed. (New York: McGraw-Hill, 1975), pp. 143-148.
3. James A. Senn, *Information System in Management* (Belmont, CA: Wadsworth Publishing Co., 1978), pp. 166-167.
4. Sanders, pp. 156-159.
5. Elias M. Awad, *Introduction to Computers in Business* (Englewood Cliffs, NJ: Prentice-Hall, Inc., 1977), pp. 115-119.
6. Awad, pp. 112-133.
7. Sanders, pp. 151-153.
8. Awad, pp. 117-118, 160-171.
9. Anthony Ralston and C.L. Meek, eds., *Encyclopedia of Computer Science* (New York: Petrocelli/Charter, 1976), pp. 667-707, 1404-1410.
10. Ralston and Meek, pp. 899-916.
11. Sanders, pp. 334-345.
12. Sanders, pp. 334-345.
13. James Martin, *An Information Systems Manifesto* (Englewood Cliffs, NJ: Prentice-Hall, Inc., 1984), p. 30.
14. Martin, pp. 31-33.
15. Ralph M. Stair, Jr., *Computers in Today's World* (Homewood, IL: Richard D. Irwin, Inc., 1986), pp. 194-210.
16. Susan J. Biedma and James Gatza, *Managing Automated Activities* (Malvern, PA: Insurance Institute of America, 1988), pp. 267-274.
17. Awad, pp. 72-76.
18. Awad, pp, 90-101.
19. Peter G. W. Keen and Lynda A. Woodman, "What To Do with All Those Micros," *Harvard Business Review*, September-October 1984, pp. 144-146.
20. John Leslie King, "Centralized versus Decentralized Computing," *Computing Surveys*, vol. 15, no. 4, December 1983, pp. 319-348.
21. King, pp. 319-348.

CHAPTER **2**

Managing the Computer

Chapter 1 described the computer and the rapid development of computer technology. Chapter 2 examines the effects of this rapid development on the people who manage computers and use the information they produce. This rapid development places tremendous demands on managers and employees. It helps to explain why even good solutions in information systems management often have a short life span.

The rapid pace of change has shifted the early focus on computer management to information management, and in recent years to the use of information systems as a vehicle for implementing an organization's strategy. Persons associated with the computer were originally charged with managing that computer. As more and more work was taken on by the computer, this approach gradually changed. Those involved in computer work began to see their jobs not as managing the computer but as managing the information of the company. Now information processing is changing again. As users become more and more comfortable with automation and personal computers, they are being challenged to take the lead in systems planning and implementation. Rather than declining in importance as a result, the role of the information systems department is evolving into that of partnership with user management. Together they provide technological leadership and guidance needed to improve the efficiency and effectiveness of the organization and to link information systems strategy with overall business strategy. As this

47

new role of information systems management continues to evolve, new challenges will arise as old ones are resolved.

COMPUTER OPERATIONS AND PEOPLE

All of us have become "computer people" to some extent. That is, everyone has had to adapt to the pervasive use of computers in business. (Personal life has not been immune to this change, but those considerations are beyond the scope of this discussion.) People now request "input" rather than the opinions of others. People now use a "systems approach"—rather than intuition—to solve problems.

People who use computers are called *users*. The term's meaning varies, however, depending on who is using it. For example, for those in the data processing department, all the other departments in the company are user departments, and all the other employees are users. From the point of view of the computer operator, however, everyone else is a user—including programmers. Adding to the confusion, computer vendors (that is, computer manufacturers) consider all their customers, including the operators, as users. To understand the specific meaning of the term, therefore, it is necessary to show it in context. Sometimes the term *end user* is used to apply to all users other than the data processing department. We will treat *user* and *end user* as synonymous.

The "computer department" of an organization is not likely to be known by that name. Rather, it may be called Information Systems, Information Services, Data Processing, Management Information Systems, Information Resources, or some other name. Perhaps the two most common labels are the initials IS and, often used out of habit, DP. The IS or DP department has probably grown steadily since its inception. There has been an impressive division of labor, too. The first uses of computers in business were usually rather simple batch-processing tasks. For example, one of the most common uses of early business computers was to replace old accounting machines that had been used to produce monthly billings. There was little need for a large staff of computer programmers, systems analysts, operators, managers, and others. But as computer power grew, more and more people were required. And as computer sophistication grew, more and more division of labor was needed. One of the first areas where this occurred was in programming. With the earliest computers, programmers actually operated the machines. After writing a program, programmers would process it on the computer, and then review the results. Soon it was realized that programmers could be more productive if all they did was write programs; someone slightly less skilled could be hired to operate the computer. As the next section will show, the computer operator's job has also gone through several divisions.

Insurance Company Computer Operations

When used in a data processing context, the term *operations* refers to the department charged with the responsibility of physical maintenance, operation, and security of the computer itself. In many companies this department is known as the *data center*. Other titles are common, such as data processing or information processing. The data center is part of the larger information systems department.

Development. Historically, operations began as part of the data processing department. The position of *operator* was considered less desirable than some of the other jobs in data processing. This was appropriate in the days prior to advanced operating systems, data communications, multiprogramming, and other features requiring significant operator activity. Picture an operator at that early time. For instance, an operator might be asked to run the monthly premium billing program. Under the previous manual system, that process might take ninety-five person-hours. The computer might take four hours for the same job. From a business perspective, this meant a dramatic increase in productivity. But from the point of view of an operator, it meant that once the data had been loaded into the computer, it was four hours before the computer could do anything else. College students often held these positions because they could study during the long operating runs and therefore accept a relatively low salary.

Change came with the advent of multiprogramming under the control of sophisticated operating systems. In addition to the four-hour job, the operator could simultaneously process other jobs on the computer. In fact, before long, additional operators were needed to keep up with the loading of punched cards and magnetic tape, and, of course, with the very frequent task of loading the printer with paper. Operations work today can require as much—or more—technical training than many programming positions.

Functions.[1] A data center, like a manufacturing operation, is set up primarily to produce output from given raw materials by utilizing equipment and consuming supplies. In fact, the term *production data processing* is often used in insurance firms to designate the high volume of routine work in a data center. The raw materials for the computer operations department or data center are the data and programs to be processed. The outputs are the required on-line services, record reports, premium notices, bills, and so on. Only the major functions involved in converting the raw materials or input into outputs will be discussed here.

Data Entry. In the past, insurance companies centralized the data entry function to convert raw data, such as policy declarations pages, into machine readable form through the use of data entry stations or other equipment. Today, with the introduction of more and more on-line applications, underwriters, raters, and claims processors are in many cases entering data directly into the computer. The need for centralized data entry facilities is being reduced significantly.

Input-Receipt. This function receives input data, prepares routing sheets, and expedites jobs. In addition, this area often serves as the user's liaison with the data center, handling questions about job status and informing users of changes in processing schedules.

Scheduling. Scheduling is the planning and control function of the data center. The basic role of the scheduling function is to provide a sequence of computer runs for a specific time period that will meet all of the deadline constraints, input availability, and task dependencies. Daily schedule revisions may be required because of system failures, reruns, emergency runs, late input, and general slippage in the run schedule. Many data centers now use computer programs to help schedule jobs by analyzing priorities, orders, hardware requirements, and resources.

Library. The library function, under the *librarian,* is responsible for the storage and control of production tapes and disks and the offsite storage of backup copies of the tapes and disks. It is also responsible for responding to requests for tape reels and disks when the jobs are prestaged for execution. The library represents a very special inventory problem. Each of the many tapes and disks is an independently identifiable inventory item which must be readily available and accounted for at all times. Without a workable plan for controlling these files, they can be misplaced, erroneously erased, or otherwise lost.

Machine Operation. This function is responsible for the operation of the machines that perform the processing of jobs and the production of output. It involves receiving media from the data conversion, input-receipt, and library functions, mounting tapes and disks, releasing jobs for processing by the computer, and controlling the job mix on a continual basis to ensure adherence to schedules.

Most large-scale systems have a computer in operation for more than the standard work day. Spreading the computer's work over two or three shifts enables a company to purchase a smaller computer than would be needed if all the computer work had to be done during the regular work day. Often there is a *lead operator,* sometimes called a *shift supervisor,* for each shift. This person directs the activities of the other operators.

Output Control and Distribution. The output control part of this function involves checking the output of a computer run for completeness and quality. In the case of batch runs, this may require checking balance totals, item counts, and print quality. For data transmissions, log sheets must be checked to ensure the completeness and accuracy of the transmission. The distribution part of the function includes responsibilities for ensuring that pages are separated, carbons removed, and sprocket holes trimmed prior to the output being sent to the end user.

Insurance Agency Computer Operations

Let us now turn from insurance company to insurance agency automation. Most agencies have some automation: the choices range from a personal computer used for a single function to a large multi-terminal minicomputer system that handles almost all information processing tasks within the agency. As a tool, automation must be managed by someone who knows the system and how it will be used in the agency. This individual is usually called the *operations manager.*

The agency operations manager is responsible for all of the data center functions described above as they apply to the agency. When a new system is installed, certain facts about the agency must be defined to the system; client and policy information must be entered; the general ledger, receivables, and payables must be loaded; and agency employees trained. File backups, periodic purges of dated information (i.e., stale prospects) and day-end, month-end, and year-end reporting runs must be scheduled into the agency's operations. Tape or disk copies of the systems' files need to be stored safely and securely in the event a disk failure requires restoration of the system from the most recent copies. Other areas of responsibility include starting the system up, shutting it down, restarting it when the system fails, resolving problems with the system's vendor, explaining new system features and functions, providing training to new employees, and maintaining the inventory of computer supplies.

In a small agency, one of the staff might be assigned the primary responsibility for operations of the computer as an additional responsibility. In large agencies, the function of operations manager may be a full-time position. No matter what the size of the agency is, however, a second person should be sufficiently trained to provide backup support whenever the primary operator is not present.

Operations Concerns

Priorities. Responsibility for managing a data center involves constant concern for priorities. Since systems design and programming resources are limited and computer power is finite, work requests must be assigned priorities. The assignment of these priorities is always a rather ticklish responsibility. End users, naturally, never think any of their jobs should be given the lowest priority and yet some projects have to be given the lowest rank. Project backlogs of many months are common in insurance firms and in business firms in general.

Processing workloads are seldom level: there are peaks and valleys over time. This is particularly true in insurance companies and agencies that have a great deal of statistical and accounting work performed once a month. Most organizations have computers large enough to take them through the expected peaks and valleys. But what if a snowstorm leads to a two-day power failure during the peak time of the month? To have enough excess computer capacity to handle every possible contingency would be an expensive luxury. But to operate the computer constantly at full capacity, without leeway for downtime, is just as costly in the long run. The solution to the problem lies in trying to strike a balance between these extremes.

The manager of computer operations often receives questions of this sort: "If the new computer can execute instructions in seconds, why is my monthly report two days late?" One likely reason is the matter of setting priorities. Priorities should emanate from the top of the organization. Naturally, the top executives of the company or agency should not have to schedule computer runs for the day, but they should establish a basic framework for setting job priorities. Perhaps priorities are established properly but are not effectively communicated throughout the organization. People can usually accept delays if those delays can be predicted to some degree and they know that their managers realize and understand the problems.

Security. At one time, executives liked to "show off" their computers. Computer rooms were frequently built like showcases with glass walls. The computer room, with all its ultra-modern equipment, was on display to anyone walking through the building. Some managers grew concerned that many of these showcase computer rooms were easy targets for protestors or for vandals. The glistening, antiseptic computer room was, for some, a symbol of the capitalist system. Moreover, it symbolized what was wrong with the system. Some of the fears were realized, and computer facilities disrupted.

In addition to the risk of damage to the equipment, managers became sensitive to the possible loss of or damage to the data stored in the computer system. Programs and tape libraries represent large investments. Firms have set up data security departments charged with the responsibility of protecting their data from sabotage by frustrated employees, disgruntled former employees, and so-called "hackers" who attempt to gain access for the sheer excitement of it.

Because of these concerns, computer rooms have become restricted areas, with entry tightly controlled. Personal identification badges and locked doors are all but standard in corporate DP areas. This heightened awareness of security is not limited to computer rooms but is conspicuously evident there. Access to data is restricted by passwords or access codes so that employees, agents, and other authorized users cannot reach data they are not intended to have. Security remains of acute importance in computer operations and is one of the major responsibilities of those charged with operations management.

Efficiency. Running an efficient data center is always an ongoing management concern. Data center efficiency is primarily a measure of how many hands-on employees, tape mounters, computer console operators, printer operators, and output distributors it has and how they are utilized. Data center efficiency can be improved by redesigning, rewriting, or replacing systems that require extensive hands-on support with systems that reduce the amount of output produced and delivered, tape mounts, console operator replys, and other manual operations. One of the first steps in improving efficiency is to create a team of operations and programming employees to identify the labor-intensive activities and the jobs that use each one of them, and then to rank the computer jobs by the amount of manual support they require. Attention can then focus on labor-intensive jobs and runs.

Systems and Programming

Once the early programmer's functions had been divided into those of programmer and operator, the stage was set for the next division, between programming and systems analysis. Further divisions have taken place, but we shall restrict ourselves to the areas of major importance.

Systems Analysts. The *systems analyst* is the data processing employee charged with the responsibility of specifying the size, scope, and characteristics of programs and systems. Although this is perhaps an adequate description of responsibility, it does not go very far towards telling us what the systems analyst does. Primary activities of a systems analyst include information gathering, design, specification, and follow-through.

Information Gathering. Suppose that an actuary wants a new kind of monthly report. Someone from the data processing department must determine precisely what the actuary wants before the programmer can write the program. One set of skills is needed when talking with users (interpersonal skills) and another set is needed when designing the program (technical skills). The systems analyst interacts with users in devising programs to meet their needs but is unlikely to do the detailed programming.

During the requirements definition phase, systems analysts interview end users to obtain information. The danger involved in relying on this approach is that it relies heavily on the user's ability to communicate what is needed and the analyst's ability to interpret what the user is saying. Each has limited knowledge of the other's field. To some extent, each speaks a different jargon. The best results come when the analyst has a solid understanding of the company's business in addition to technical data processing knowledge.[2]

Design. Once sufficient information has been gathered, the systems analyst begins with the design of the program or system. In fact, systems analysts rarely design individual programs. They design a system and then programs within that system's context. It often takes several programs to perform what looks, to a user, to be one function. For instance, in the case of using the computer to issue workers compensation policies, four programs may be involved—one to rate policies, another to print policies, a third to format the data for a statistical report, and a fourth for accounting.

Specification. Once the system design has been determined, the systems analyst gives the programmer documents that describe or specify what the system must do and the manner in which it must be done. These are called the specifications and usually take the form of data flow diagrams, decision tables, and print and screen layouts.

Data Flow Diagrams. A data flow diagram depicts a system in terms of its components and their interrelationships or interfaces among these components. As Exhibit 2-1 illustrates, the basic data flow diagram uses just four symbols:

- A square to designate a source and/or destination of data outside the system, an agency or an agency's customer.

Exhibit 2-1
Policy Processing Data Flow Diagram

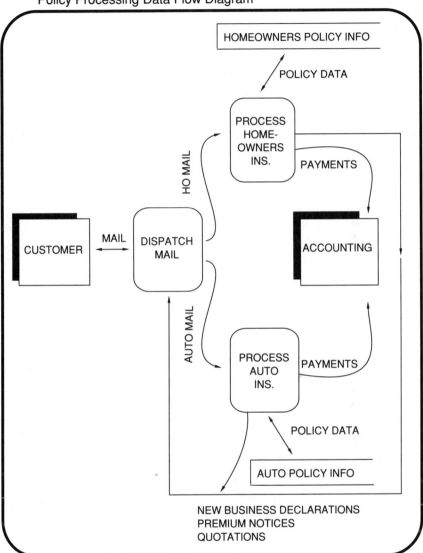

- An arrow to show how information moves into, around, and out of the system.
- A rectangle with rounded corners to indicate a process in the system that changes the data in some way.
- An open-ended rectangle to show a place in the process where information is stored in some way.

Data flow diagrams include manual tasks in addition to those that are to be automated.

Decision Tables. A *decision table* is a matrix that shows the decisions to be made in processing data. The decisions take the form of IF-THEN statements. The matrix first lists the conditions that may occur, (IF customer account balance is 0; IF customer account balance is greater than 0; IF customer account balance is less than 0) and then, below, lists the actions that are to be taken (THEN go to next record; THEN go to billing routine; THEN go to refund routine). To the right of both conditions and actions are places for x's at various points on the matrix. These x's indicate which actions correspond to which conditions. Decision tables are desirable for programs involving complicated branching.

Print and Screen Layouts. Unfortunately, computers cannot simply be told to print or display the "premiums on the left, losses on the right, and totals at the bottom." In the past, spacing charts were used to produce reports or display information. Today, automated screen and report format programs are used to design reports and screens, in many cases by the end users. The formats generated by these programs can be input directly into the application program, rather than being recoded by a programmer.

Follow-Through. This is probably the most time-consuming of all the activities of the systems analyst. Follow-through includes many things: answering the questions of the programmer; assisting in or even directing the implementation of a new system; answering the questions of users and resolving errors (bugs) in the new-system; and any related tasks. The systems analyst is often a jack-of-all-trades, spending as much time maintaining and improving old systems as designing new ones.

Programmers. The *programmer* creates and tests the instructions that the computer executes. Primary activities of a programmer include program writing, debugging, testing, documentation, and maintenance.

Program Writing. Using the language selected by the organization, the programmer codes (or writes) a program to accomplish a data processing task. In most instances, the programmer will begin with a flowchart showing major calculation steps. Programs are seldom written in isolation; instead, they are designed to interface with existing programs. Often the organization's program library contains program modules for commonly performed functions.

Debugging. Errors in programs are called *bugs* and the process of correcting them carries the now-familiar name, *debugging.* Most programmers write or "code" their programs directly on a terminal or personal computer. At this point, the program is ready to be compiled. The compiler, itself a program, translates the program into machine language that the computer can internally process. Before making the translation, however, it checks for certain errors (each programming language has a syntax that must be followed by the programmer). Errors found are shown on a printout. The programmer then locates these errors and corrects them. The program can then be compiled again. This process is repeated until the compiler detects no errors. At that time the program is fully translated into machine language and stored in the computer as an *object program.* The precompiled program, called a *source program,* is stored for use if changes are required later.

Testing.   The next step is to test the program by running test data. For example, if the program is to rate automobile insurance policies, sample policies will be converted to an input medium and run through the program. Results of the program are reviewed. Errors found at this stage are also called bugs and the debugging process continues. The success of the program may depend on the diversity, depth, and volume of the test data used to test it. The more varied the test data, the less likely that "unforeseen" problems will develop in the future.   This is especially true if programs are individually tested, then tested as part of the whole system, and then put through an acceptance test by the end user.

Documentation.   If a programmer could remember every program he or she ever wrote, the structure of every program, and the location of every instruction of the program, and agreed to remain with the company as long as his or her programs remained in use, then there would be little need for documentation. *Documentation* involves preparation of a permanent record of each program or system. It can take the form of flow charts, decision tables, narrative charts, or other written depiction. Documentation is prepared either before the program is completed, after the program is finished, or, at times, during the programming process.   It is probably the least pleasurable of all of the phases of programming, but the need for it is obvious and becomes apparent each time a program must be modified.

Maintenance.   All changes to a program, whether they are corrections or improvements, are called program *maintenance.* If program maintenance were unnecessary, then program documentation to a large degree would be unnecessary. Today, most major business organizations have a major investment in computer programs, and large sums are spent annually to maintain them. New programs often incorporate preexisting ones or their output; properly maintained programs are an obvious benefit as new information needs emerge.

Applications Programming vis-a-vis Systems Programming. The distinction made in Chapter 1 between applications software and systems software also applies to applications programming and systems programming.

An *applications programmer* works on business problems. In the case of an insurance agency, the applications programmer works on programs related to the agency's business, such as accounts receivable, accounts current, policyholder files, and related programs. Applications programmers normally use procedure-oriented languages, although they are by no means restricted to these.

Systems programmers primarily work with operating system software. This being the case, most of their work is done in symbolic language. There is a trend, however, toward the use of some higher level languages in systems software. One of the prime reasons for this is that systems programmers are scarce. Writing systems software in higher level languages qualifies many others for the field of systems programming.

Development Programming vis-a-vis Maintenance Programming. Some *shops* (the buzzword for data processing departments) organize programmers into development and maintenance staffs. Development programming is concerned with programs that are being written for the first time—either applications programs or systems programs. Operating systems software is for the most part written by the computer manufacturer or a firm that specializes in it. In contrast, applications programming offers many opportunities for development work and is generally thought to offer greater recognition. Paradoxically, though, the more development programming that is done, the greater the amount of maintenance programming that will be required in the future.

Maintenance programming includes correcting, improving, and sometimes even overhauling existing programs and systems. Although it suffers from lower status, it is of crucial importance. It may be tolerable to fall several days behind in development (that new report for the claims department). It may not be acceptable to report delays in maintenance (correct the program that prints the claims drafts for policyholders).

Trends. The distinctions between systems analysis and programming outlined above are valid from a conceptual point of view. In terms of specific job descriptions, however, the picture has become increasingly blurred with time.

Historically, systems analysts were programmers who had been promoted. Gradually, it was recognized that the two jobs required different skills. Consequently, some organizations offered a career path for programmers that did not necessitate a switch to systems analysis.

Still, in terms of status, systems analysis was considered preferable to development programming, much as development programming was preferable to maintenance programming. To combat this tendency, some companies combined the two positions to create the position of *programmer analyst.*

Many companies chose to alter the structure even more dramatically by taking a project management approach. With this approach, programmers and analysts are assigned to a specific major project and remain members of that project's group for its duration. Project management does not replace the traditional structure but usually exists in addition to it. Many software projects are of sufficient complexity and duration to warrant project management.

The Database Administrator. Database processing is a technique for organizing and manipulating integrated data. For example, in a database application, producer, policy, and claim data records can be integrated into a single database. Relationships among these records are represented in the database, and these relationships are used to process the data. As a result it is possible to retrieve all of the policies and their respective claims, if any, for a given producer or to determine the name of the producer who sold a particular policy resulting in a claim.

More than any other single person, the database administrator (DBA) controls the success or failure of the database approach in an organization. The DBA is the custodian of the organization's data. Being a custodian of data is very different from being the owner of the data. Just as the manager of a bank is responsible for the safety of what is in the bank's vault, the database administrator is responsible for safekeeping and controlling the organization's data. This responsibility includes the establishment of standards for the format of data and files within the computer system, modifying file and data relationships, and adding record types or modifying an old record to contain new data. These tasks require knowledge of systems analysis, programming, operations management, and a thorough knowledge of the organization's data and therefore its business. Because of these extensive knowledge requirements, the database administrator is usually a department or group rather than one person.

Managing Data Processing Professionals. [3] People who work in the information systems or data processing profession are often presumed to have basic characteristics different from those associated with other professions because some of the complexity and mystique of computers has been imputed to the people who work with them. Data processing professionals deal with the same problems on the job—communication problems, staffing problems, disenchantment with the "boss," lack of motivation, and job turnover—that all employees encounter at one time or another in their careers. The challenge for IS managers, as well as for all managers in general, is to provide an environment in which individuals and teams can be effective. Such an environment emphasizes the following:

- quality to give employees pride in what they do;
- dividing work into segments such that the delivery of each piece provides the individual or team with the reassurance and satisfaction that they are performing satisfactorily;
- encouraging successful project teams to stay together in order to channel the momentum developed in prior projects into each successive assignment; and
- free-flowing lines of communication between users and information systems employees to provide them with the background needed to appreciate how their work affects the organization's business objectives.

As is true of all employees, in addition to having a motivational environment, data processing employees must also be counseled, evaluated, and rewarded. Some of their jobs have become dull and routine. Computer specialists often identify more strongly with the IS profession than with the insurance industry. Systems staff development, as noted below, must encompass the traditional technical subjects, as well as increasing the interpersonal skills necessary for information systems employees to be perceived as partners by their users.

Systems Staff Development.[4] Traditionally, information systems departments have focused their training efforts on increasing the technical skills of the IS staff. Increased competitiveness in the insurance industry, the increased pace of technological change in information systems, and the growing computer literacy of end users now place more emphasis on human resource skills and on developing both a basic understanding of general business and a knowledge of the insurance industry, its products, services, and operations. At the same time, the technical skills that systems professionals must learn continue to increase. In addition to the core systems skills, systems employees must learn how to use new development and maintenance programmer productivity improvement tools, new analysis and design techniques, new programming languages, local area networks, and expert system technologies. Learning how to use these new technologies is only part of the challenge. The other part is learning how to identify potential applications within the user areas to which these technologies can be applied and then being able to market these solutions to the users and senior management.

IS personnel need interpersonal and general management skills if they are to be considered part of the company's management group. Interpersonal skills training for information systems professionals often focuses on improving negotiation skills with users; building positive, long-term relationships with users, co-workers, and management; developing job and career goal-setting skills; managing time and stress; and enhancing business-oriented oral and written communication skills. General management skill development is always a critical development need for those systems employees in management and project management career paths. In the past, systems professionals have often been promoted into management because of their success as technicians. If this happens without their knowing how to manage, there is a greater likelihood that the new managers will not do as well as they or their managers would like because of the natural tendency to continue focusing on the technical aspects of the work rather than achieving the appropriate mix of technical and general management expertise required to perform as managers. Management training for system professionals in the general management and project management career paths should begin before they are promoted to management positions. In addition to general management skills, future managers need the industry and organizational knowledge noted above. This knowledge is necessary for managers to clearly state and negotiate the purpose and scope of a project or discuss the use of new technologies to solve business problems in a nontechnical manner with user management.

Fourth-generation languages, discussed in Chapter 1, should be cited again as a trend. These languages offer two major benefits. First, they allow users to produce their own programs, thus saving time. Second, programmers are freed from time-consuming chores. For example, writing programs to create reports are rarely challenging assignments for programmers. Thus, programmers and users both are happy to see the introduction of report writer software in the organization.

Computer Vendors

The term *vendors* includes hardware manufacturers and manufacturers that sell hardware and software together. When the first computers were sold, the computer itself was the entire product. In time, manufacturers added operating systems software to the computer.

Since the first generation, many other services have emerged to fill particular needs of computer buyers. One can now obtain the services of programmers without hiring them (contract programming), or obtain complete packages of programs already written.

Computer vendors range from someone with a personal lines rating system for sale to International Business Machines (IBM), one of the largest corporations in the world. Some vendors offer only one highly specialized service, while others offer a wide range of products and services.

Our discussion of vendors will be in terms of their major products or services, even though they may offer others as well. For example, although IBM is mentioned in the section on hardware vendors, this does not mean IBM sells no software.

The discussion now turns to vendors and the services they offer. This discussion will help portray the options available to satisfy data processing needs. Many organizations have purchased a particular product or service as a result of an initial inquiry by a user. Moreover, many vendors, aware that this happens, seek to make contact with user managers. Indeed, in some cases vendors avoid going through the information processing staff as they promote their wares to users.

Hardware Vendors. Who has not heard of IBM? The name is virtually synonymous with computers. And yet, IBM is by no means the "only game in town." Hardware vendors can be surveyed in terms of a number of classifications—by type of equipment, by size of equipment, by customer, and by additional services offered.

Type of Equipment. Some companies produce all types of computer equipment—from the central processing unit to terminals and everything in between. Others produce only certain types of machines. For example, many companies got started in the 1960s by offering peripherals (everything but the central processing unit) that could be used with IBM computers. These were called *plug-compatibles,* referring to the fact that they could be plugged directly into IBM equipment. Some of these manufacturers achieved enviable success by specializing. They avoided the need to provide many of the services that IBM offered its customers and were therefore able to sell their products at low prices. Some of these companies, due to specialization, were able to offer superior products.

Size of Equipment. Widespread use of minicomputers and

microcomputers has been spearheaded by companies that specialize in their use and programs. For a while, minicomputer manufacturers were considered to be in a separate category from "standard" computer manufacturers. This is no longer true, since many manufacturers of large computers also offer minicomputers and microcomputers. Other manufacturers produce only one model of a personal computer. Most hardware makers, however, tend to emphasize a particular product line over others and eventually find that IBM has become a competitor if a particular product appears profitable.

Customer. Some hardware vendors tend to pursue a particular class of customer. Customers cannot be divided simply into two categories—scientific users and business users. Market segmentation is more complex than this. For instance, some manufacturers strive to reach the "sophisticated data processing user" with their "technically superior equipment." Others may cater to general business customers. Still others may seek out the "high technology" business equipment designed for such use. The approaches represent differences in the nature of the equipment as well as in marketing strategies.

Services in Addition to Equipment. Some vendors will put service representatives into the user organization on a full-time basis. In contrast, other companies sell their equipment by mail or telephone. Many of the hardware vendors that followed the pioneers declined at first to offer many of the additional services provided by the established vendors. Over time, many have added services and products to compete with long-established vendors. These services and products include contract programming, contract systems analysis, education and training, other consulting, and perhaps most significant, operating systems software. Much of the plug-compatible equipment sold today is designed to operate with IBM software and is sold without systems software.

Software Vendors. During the 1950s, some companies began to provide contract programming services. These were often one or two person firms and many had one major client, the federal government. This came about as salaries for programmers rose well above authorized pay levels for programmers within the government. As a consequence, federal government agencies contracted a great deal of their programming work to outside firms.[5] From this origin, programming vendors expanded and offered programs and systems of programs *(software packages)* to additional customers with little incremental cost. This was the basis for what we call today the *software house.* (Note that while a software vendor is also called a software house, a hardware vendor is never called a hardware house.)

Some software houses maintain contract programming work as an integral product offering. Others will develop packages on speculation and then seek customers. Many do both. Some vendors specialize in systems software while others restrict their activities to the applications level.

Advantages of Purchased Software.

Some software houses place major emphasis on the software needs of the insurance industry. These efforts appear beneficial to both vendors and customers. Nonetheless, some insurance executives maintain that software is best developed in-house. Some of the advantages reputed to accrue to those who purchase their applications software include saving programmers, time, and money.[6]

Saves Staff. The demand for programmers, systems analysts, and IS administrators has kept well ahead of supply, bidding up the price of their labor. In addition, the maintenance of existing systems has been estimated to consume most of the programmer's time and represents as much as 70 percent of all software expenses. If a software package can be purchased, the buying company may not require many, if any, additional programmers. Programmers currently on the company's staff may be used to maintain and rebuild older systems. Within a small organization, such as an agency, purchasing software similarly means a saving in someone's time.

Saves Time. Buying software often means buying programs that have already been written, debugged, and are ready for immediate use. If the work were to be done in-house, implementation of the system would be delayed until all the programming was completed. This could mean a saving of months or even years in the case of full function commercial lines rating and policy processing systems.

Saves Money. Since the software house sells or hopes to sell a particular system to many companies, the development cost is usually spread among many customers. Few, if any, agencies and brokers would be able to pay for the development of a customized agency automation system.

Disadvantages of Purchased Software.

Shortcomings of Purchased Software. Arguments against the use of purchased software usually point out that some of the benefits cited above are not realized with some systems. This stands more as an argument against a particular package or against a particular vendor than as a criticism of the concept of software packages.

Problems of Integration. Another frequent objection carries greater weight—the contention that packages often do not easily fit with the procedures of the purchasing company. When this happens, the purchasing company must either modify the package or change its business practices. Excessive modification defeats the advantage of buying packaged software.

Today there is a whole spectrum of software applications available to the insurance industry. Agencies can purchase complete agency management systems for multiple tasks or specific software packages to perform specific tasks such as quotations or marketing. Insurance companies have access to personal and commercial lines policy processing, billing, claims, management information, and agency/company interface software packages. The biggest problem facing the industry now is not deciding whether to "make or buy" but determining what the organization's business requirements are and which software package comes closest to meeting business needs.

Other Vendors. Other vendors in the computer industry—communications carriers, facilities management firms, service bureaus, remote processing operations, and time sharing firms—combine features of hardware and software vendors.

Communications Carriers. Communications carriers provide the means for computer users to establish computer networks. The presence of a remote terminal implies the presence of a communications link, usually a leased telephone line or circuit. The most obvious example is the American Telephone and Telegraph Company. Another illustration is the IBM Information Network that provides network services to IVANS. Other private networks have also been established. The use of space satellites has increased the opportunity for other firms to compete in the field of data transmission. As computer networks proliferate, this market is expected to grow in importance and in the range of services offered.

Facilities Management Firms. A facilities management arrangement usually involves subcontracting the entire data processing function. The facilities management firm staffs, purchases, and controls all computer equipment. Since this approach requires total reliance on one outside firm, it has not enjoyed widespread use within the insurance industry.

Service Bureaus. Service bureaus differ from facilities management firms in that they seldom take total responsibility for the data processing function of the customer. They provide contract systems analysis, perform some data entry functions, contract programming, and perform the production runs. Their responsibilities include only those tasks they have agreed to perform as opposed to a broad mandate to accomplish the entire data processing function. Insurance agencies have long been served by service bureaus that began by offering batch processing but in some instances now sell agency computer systems.

Remote Processing Facilities. Remote processing can be performed by a service bureau, software house, or other firm. It requires the installation of computer terminals at the customer's location. The software is provided by the vendor—usually an applications system of some sort. The responsibility of the vendor covers the proper and necessary operation of the software package and sometimes the equipment itself but seldom goes beyond this. Remote processing is of benefit when a customer wants a software package but does not want to install the package or have the problems associated with operating a computer. Remote processing stops short of facilities management since it usually leaves hardware responsibility to the customer, is limited to a particular system or set of systems to be operated, and utilizes a CPU at the vendor's site.

Timesharing Firms. Although not as popular as they once were, timesharing firms provide service to a significant number of users. This service involves placing remote terminals at the customer site. Each customer has complete access to the computer and appears to have exclusive use of the computer. Of course, this is not actually true, but delays are negligible as the computer processes work for a number of users simultaneously. Timesharing does allow the customer to do programming at a terminal. Thus, timesharing does not restrict the user to specific systems in the way remote processing does.

Others. There are still other firms offering computing and communications services similar, but not identical, to those described above. Variations are likely to continue as each firm tries to establish a unique market. Further proliferation of services and vendors is expected.

Selecting Vendor Services. Users of computer services should be informed about the options available to the data processing or information systems department. Detailed examination of any product or service, and an ultimate verdict on its merit from a data processing point of view, remain the responsibility of information processing specialists. However, data processing personnel cannot pass judgment on the value of computer services to users without consulting them. Informed users and knowledgeable specialists must work together in assessing cost/benefits and quality consideration of alternative ways of meeting user needs.

Users of Computers

As noted previously, the terms *user* and *end user* both designate the person or unit that receives the results of a computer run.

Growing Dependence. Users continue to grow more and more dependent on computers. When an insurer puts an agency's account balances on the computer so that the monthly accounts can be computer-prepared, all future references to the account balance will require the use of the computer. Personal computers are widely used in the home, at school, and at work. Advertisements expound the virtues of personal computers. Automatic teller machines (ATMs) are used to complete banking transactions. Scanners and related technology are used to process purchases in many retail stores. There is nothing in sight that appears to have any chance of reversing the trend toward increased dependence on automation.

This mounting dependence requires that end users become more knowledgeable about the computer systems that affect them as well as obtaining tools (such as those provided by the information center discussed below) to satisfy most of their information needs.

Computing in User Departments. One of the major issues senior IS and insurance executives must resolve is control over computing—who does it, what they do with it, and how.

Until the introduction of personal computers, data processing departments controlled the availability of information. With the increasing number of articles and advertisements touting the availability of technology and its ease of use, the increasing proliferation of micros and the growing number of new employees with some experience in PC operation, insurance company employees increasingly believe they can participate in the information processing revolution by taking back some of the tasks historically performed by IS. This is especially true if they feel they need or can obtain the needed information faster than the IS department can provide it.

Data processing departments are often criticized for their slow response to new requests for information. Some IS departments face application request backlogs of a year or more. There are many reasons for this. Skilled systems analysts and programmers are scarce. They often have higher turnover than others in the company, which disrupts IS project schedules and budgets. Within the insurance industry changing state regulations, product and rate revisions, and one-time requests for information create a heavy maintenance workload, consuming resources that could otherwise be assigned to new application development projects. Programming projects compete against other uses of funds within IS and in other departments when organizational budgets are set. Some insurers find that the fastest way to break the maintenance log jam is to give the requesters of new information the tools to obtain the information themselves.

Information Center. The objective of the *information center* is to provide do-it-yourself help for insurance professionals to meet many of their information requirements. The information center is not the place where employees walk in to order new applications. Complex production tasks are still channeled to the IS department where they belong, while the information center handles simple business applications. The information center provides aid to the full range of information users, helping them solve their own problems. The center may allow insurance professionals to pose questions, often a series of questions using sophisticated programming languages, against the large volumes of mainframe data characteristic of insurance companies. The center offers the ability to analyze options; to create and maintain manuals, reports, directories, graphs, charts, memos, notes, and letters; to obtain self-paced training in appropriate software and hardware tools; and to develop models for presentation and evaluation of alternatives, simulating operations, and testing contingencies.

Information centers benefit insurance and IS professionals in many ways. By absorbing simple business applications and maintenance tasks, information centers can relieve the IS department of much of the crippling programming backlogs they currently face and free resources for developing complex application systems such as commercial lines policy processing and office and underwriting systems. Information centers allow IS departments to retain control of information resources, while extending IS support throughout the organization and reducing much of the friction between IS and the rest of the company. Increased self-sufficiency in data processing also helps insurance professionals accelerate the response time to their information needs while improving the quality, completeness and timeliness of that response. By learning firsthand the problems associated with the development of new computer applications, insurance professionals become more proficient at defining their requirements to the IS department and more understanding of the problems faced by the IS department during the development of complex information systems.

Telecommuting. Microcomputers and advances in telecommunications have made it possible to move office jobs out of expensive urban headquarters to the suburbs and sometimes into an employee's home. *Telecommuting* and *electronic cottage* are two of the terms used to describe arrangements in which employees stay home all or most of the time and use a computer terminal or microcomputer to process messages, mail, assignments, and reports, and communicate the results to the home office. Advocates cite several advantages. Time consuming and often nervewracking trips to and from the office are avoided. Because telecommuting requires little mobility, it offers special opportunities to people whose physical handicaps make it difficult to work in a typical office. The overhead costs of providing parking lots, primary work space, and lunch rooms would also be reduced. Productivity is expected to increase on the assumption that employees will work with fewer interruptions.

As is true with any new method of working, people cannot be thrown into this novel work arrangement without preparation. Managers will have to set productivity goals and cost criteria. Managers must also establish quality standards for the work to be done and criteria for selecting persons to work at home. To be productive at home, a worker must be a self starter and free of interruptions, especially from children.

Companies implementing work-at-home programs will have to keep these workers in touch with the office by bringing them in for meetings, training, and celebrations to build and maintain the teamwork and commitment necessary for an organization's success. It is too soon to know how successful telecommuting will be in the insurance industry.

Becoming Comfortable with Automation. Employees have many misconceptions about the impact of automation on their jobs. One misconception many people have is that they will be required to have a much greater knowledge of mathematics to use computers. Most users have no need to use mathematical procedures. When there is a need, it is usually satisfied by a basic knowledge of math. Another misconception is the perceived need to know a computer language. Automation will probably not require many workers to develop sophisticated skills. The newest software uses plain English so effectively that learning takes only a few hours. Many first-time users of computer equipment are afraid that they will not be able to develop all of the skills needed to operate the computer safely and will destroy a program or break the computer by pressing the wrong key. The latest office computers and terminals are specifically designed to require no special operating skills. In many cases playing with the keyboard for a few minutes eliminates this concern. Some people fear that they will not learn to use a computer and thus become members of a new class of labor, the computer illiterate. Other concerns include losing their job, and in the case of middle managers, losing status in the organization because of the loss of staff and the loss of their ability to gather and process information. Employees facing automation for the first time often wonder if they will still be as valuable as before and if they will be able to keep up with their younger colleagues.

The question of health hazards associated with the use of computer equipment ranks as a major issue. Some states are considering legislation with provisions for transferring pregnant employees from work requiring computer screens. Unions see the health hazard issue as an aid in obtaining recognition or concessions. No conclusive evidence exists that computer terminals pose health hazards to pregnant women who operate them. A National Institute for Occupational Safety and Health study concluded that radiation surveys of computer screens demonstrated that exposure to X-ray, radio-frequency, ultraviolet, and visible radiation was well below current occupational exposure standards, and, in many cases, below the detection capability of the survey instruments. Air samples showed that there were no hazardous chemical exposures. [7] Nevertheless, recent reports of pregnancy problems among computer operators in the U.S. and Canada are of concern to many and have resulted in further studies.

Fatigue is a significant issue. Fatigue—eye strain, swollen muscles, and back, arm and wrist pain—can be the result of improperly designed workstations. In addition, emotional problems such as anxiety, depression, and anger tend to arise when users of terminals feel isolated from their co-workers, or feel that their work contributes less than it did under manual methods, or that the computer is monitoring their work. Solutions to these problems are available from the field of *ergonomics*. Ergonomics is the study of anatomical, physiological, and psychological aspects of people in their working environments. Exhibit 2-2 illustrates the ergonomic considerations of the computer workstation.

Making Users More Effective. [8] Phrases such as "doing the right things right" often become overused and meaningless slogans, because they are not clearly understood by the employees who are expected to adopt and apply them to their work. The right things are activities that support the achievement of an insurance organization's business objectives. Activities improving effectiveness—doing things right—include increasing profitability through a reduction in underwriting expenses, reducing expenses per person in an agency, increasing sales, and providing better services to the organization's agents, policyholders, and employees.

Information systems can also help make end users more effective by helping them reduce activities that do not contribute to their company's business objectives. These activities include correcting errors, adjusting to delays, and performing unproductive tasks. The first step in reducing errors is to identify them and their causes. Once the cause is identified, a new information system can be designed or an existing one modified to correct the error. Expert systems assist insurance compa-

Exhibit 2-2
Ergonomic Considerations of a VDT Workstation*

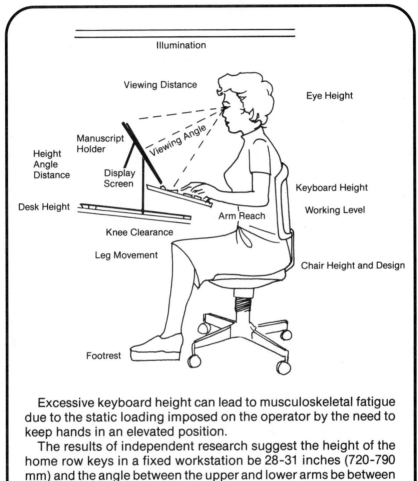

Excessive keyboard height can lead to musculoskeletal fatigue due to the static loading imposed on the operator by the need to keep hands in an elevated position.

The results of independent research suggest the height of the home row keys in a fixed workstation be 28-31 inches (720-790 mm) and the angle between the upper and lower arms be between 80° and 120°. This would require the keyboard to be approximately elbow height.

*Reprinted with permission from *Workers' Compensation Bulletin,* American Insurance Association.

nies in the consistent application of their underwriting policies throughout the field offices to reduce the adverse affect of underwriting oversights on the company's loss ratio. Delays in creating documents, mail delivery delays, and in-basket delays are common in the insurance industry. To reduce processing delays, the industry is developing information systems that cross organizational boundaries. Agency/company interface, discussed in detail in Chapter 3, is one example of systems that reduce processing delays and cross organizational boundaries. Others include electronic transfer of annual statement data between insurance companies and insurance regulators and the distribution of industry-wide statistics, loss data, and forms to insurance companies on machine-readable media. Electronic mail is used to reduce the time spent in "telephone tag" and other unproductive activities. As commercial lines masterfile systems mature, as claims and policy data is integrated using database technology, and more and more statistical data is made available online, unproductive time spent looking for information in policy files and in stacks of computer output will be significantly reduced.

More effective ways of doing things are evolving and becoming possible as a result of elimination of unnecessary activities such as those noted here. When an insurance organization reduces the cost of errors, delays, and unproductive activities, it is then in a position to invest some of the savings in projects that will improve its ability to meet its business objectives.

Insurance Work in the Future. As noted earlier, for most of the computer era, computers have been primarily used to reduce clerical costs. With the advent of personal computers in the early 1980s, automation began to touch almost every job and it should not be long before most insurance industry employees are using personal computers at their desks. Local area networks will connect their PCs with other PCs, mainframes, and large databases to provide automation support for a group of employees, rather than just one person. The most likely result of these interconnected PCs will be a change in the nature of the jobs in the section, department, or work group, making jobs more effective by reducing turn-around time for creating the unit's particular work products. As noted above, the time saved can then be spent performing more important activities such as direct customer contact with agents, policyholders, and claimants.

The nature of managerial work will also change. Until recently, management received computer printouts showing summarized results. Now, fourth generation languages and on-line databases allow managers to analyze the information on their terminals and PCs from a number of different perspectives. These new information systems will give the organization's managers better control of the business by allowing them to identify trends earlier and to obtain enough information to improve and feel more confident with the decisions they will have to make.

INFORMATION RESOURCE MANAGEMENT

In this section, attention shifts from the people involved with the computer to management processes that are affected by it. Although some of the same facts will be cited, the issues will be of a different nature. Thus far, emphasis has been on individual reactions to the widespread use of computers. The rest of the chapter will emphasize organizational reactions to the same phenomenon.

Information: Costs and Value [9]

In recent years, as the perspective shifted from computer management to information management, there was a corollary adjustment from cost-benefit analysis of the computer to a cost-benefit analysis of information. The costs and benefits are taken broadly, from the viewpoint of users as well as of top executives.

Cost of Information. The cost of obtaining, or capturing, information, can be divided into the following five general categories.

1. *Cost of Hardware.* Since the cost of the hardware is the price actually paid for purchase or lease of equipment, it is probably the easiest figure to derive.

2. *Cost of Software.* This includes all program development costs and the cost of purchased software.

3. *Cost for Space and Environment Control Factors.* This includes floor space, preparation, special temperature and humidity controls, and power control units. With large-scale computers, these costs can be significant.

4. *Cost of Conversion.* This category includes both the one-time cost associated with conversion from a manual procedure to a computerized procedure and the cost of upgrading or converting from one computer system to another. The conversion cost is often considerably higher than the total costs of hardware, installation, and program development.

5. *Cost of Operation.* This category includes the personnel, supplies, space, utilities, and other costs associated with the maintenance and operation of the information management function.

Value of Information. Unlike the cost information, the value of information is extremely difficult to quantify and must be approached almost exclusively from a conceptual point of view. The value of information is based on the following:

1. *Accessibility.* How easily and quickly can the information be accessed? It may be a matter of seconds through a PC or terminal, or a matter of hours through some batch method.

2. *Comprehensiveness.* Not how voluminous, but how comprehensive is the information in question? Does it provide answers to a broad range of managerial and nonmanagerial questions?

3. *Accuracy.* To what degree is the information free from error? (Since no human information is infallible, an error rate, however small, is inevitable.)

4. *Appropriateness.* Is the information tailored to the needs of users?

5. *Timeliness.* How much time elapses from the input of information into the system until the output is available to the user? Is information available when needed for activities and decisions?

6. *Clarity.* Can the inexperienced or occasional user understand it without aid?

7. *Flexibility.* How flexible is the information in its use? Can it be used for more than one decision, or by more than one decision maker?

8. *Verifiability.* Can the information be verified easily?

9. *Freedom from Bias.* Is the information free from any attempt to alter or modify it in order to support a preconceived conclusion? (If information has been "screened," its objectivity, and therefore value, has been reduced.)

There are trade-offs among these elements of the value of information. If near-perfect accuracy is to be achieved, timeliness is likely to suffer. Comprehensiveness may be increased by sacrificing appropriateness. The right mix of costs and values should reflect the organization's strategy, objectives, and climate.

Information Management Concepts

Data and Information.[10] Up to this point, this text has used the terms data and information interchangeably, as they often are used in everyday speech. Those involved in information processing make a clear distinction between data and information. *Data* is defined as recorded facts or figures that have no meaning without knowledge of the context they will be used in. A listing of policies and premiums is an example of data. *Information* is knowledge obtained from data. A summation of premium volume by agency showing the premium produced during the last quarter by each agent is an example of information.

The distinction between data and information suggests the possibility that information systems can be filled with data, but provide inadequate information. It is not uncommon for some computer installations to produce reports that go unread. The problem is usually labeled *information overkill:* swamping the manager with data or insufficiently refined information. As a result, asking the right questions assumes central importance during the gathering of system requirements. The focus must be on formulating sound questions—ones that result in the provision of information that permits a greater understanding and control of the organization.

Information Management and Management Information System. These ostensibly synonymous terms mean quite different things.

Information Management. The term information management means the management of information within the organization. It refers to the manager's concern with the creation, flow, and use of information throughout the organization. Managers involved with computers have shifted the focus from "computer management" to "information management."

Management Information. Management is the modifier in this term. Thus management information specifies a particular type of information—information used by managers or for managerial purposes. To illustrate, an insurer's information system contains many items of claims information. Some of these items, perhaps in summarized form, are useful to the persons who supervise claims activity. Other items can be regarded as technical details used by adjusters but not channeled to claims managers for their supervisory functions. The distinction between technical information and management information is based primarily on the decisions to be made on the basis of the information rather than on the kind of information. Management information reflects the need to extract from a mass of information those items that are needed by managers, the result of a process of selecting, summarizing, and presenting information needed for managerial decisions.

Management Information System. The *management information system (MIS)* has been one of the most talked about and written about subjects in the field of management over the last decades. Few students or even occasional readers of management periodicals would fail to recognize the initials MIS. It has a good image in some circles and an unsavory one in others.

One of the dilemmas facing those who seek to understand more about MIS is that there is no universally accepted definition of what one is. Logically, we might be able to modify the general definition of a system to say that an MIS is a set of management information components that interact with one another for some management purpose. The following, however, is more representative of the definitions used in MIS literature. It describes an MIS as:

> A group of people, a set of manuals, and data processing equipment
> that select, store, process, and retrieve data to reduce the uncertainty
> in decision-making by yielding information for managers at the time
> they can most efficiently use it. [11]

This definition suggests that the ultimate purpose in using an MIS is the reduction of uncertainty—something insurance people can understand! But the reference is to a particular type of uncertainty—the type associated with making decisions. Implicit in this part of the definition is the assumption that uncertainty in decision making can and should be reduced. An MIS, therefore, can be judged on the basis of how it reduces uncertainty in management decision making. Those with insurance backgrounds will be cautious in judging an MIS since there can be a difference between perceived and actual uncertainty. [12]

The definition further states that the way an MIS reduces uncertainty in decision making is by providing information. So it is clear that an MIS is expected to yield information, not data.

The definition goes on to point out that the information must be provided when the manager can most efficiently use it.

The definition does not say that an MIS is limited to what the computer does. It does not even say that a computer is the focal point of the system. It simply mentions data processing equipment as one of the elements of the MIS. Of course, as a practical matter, a computer is normally assumed to be the central component of any MIS.

Information System. It may seem odd to describe the general term *information system* after the more specific one *management information system*. There is a reason for this. MIS is probably more widely used and many attempts have been made to establish its essential meaning. In fact, the term will usually appear in capital letters when in print, in its abbreviated form. Information system, on the other hand, always appears in lower case: the term is now considered generic. Information system is a rather imprecise term embracing the creation, processing, and use of information in the organization. The label information system usually signifies concern for the entire organization, not just management. Paying too little attention to the distinction between the broader universe (the information system) and the narrower domain (the MIS) may result in computer systems that fail to meet all of the organization's key information needs.

CHALLENGES IN MANAGING INFORMATION

The information services manager of today's business organization faces some difficult challenges. Most of them involve keeping up with the demands of constant change.

Achieving Integration—Balancing User and IS Responsibilities

The role of IS and its relationship with end users continues to change. As users develop expertise in the use of personal computers, they tend to develop expectations that differ from those of people whose main exposure to computers has been the mainframe. These experienced users do not ask if something can be done; they expect that it can be done and think that it should be easy to develop and implement. As user frustrations with the perceived lack of IS responsiveness and their expectations of and familiarity with computers grow, so do their requests to take on additional responsibilities throughout the development of new systems.

The challenge for information systems management is to develop the credibility with their end users to overcome user perceptions that the only way to get more out of systems is to use PCs and to do some of the programming themselves. Improving responsiveness to user requests can be one very effective way to overcome this perceived lack of performance. Discovering what is important to end users involves understanding the user's operations and business objectives and then working with them to identify and prioritize their automation projects.

Supporting Strategic Objectives

Historically, top executives of many companies have tended to look on data processing primarily as a support function for performing routine accounting and clerical operations. This view sometimes lingers even after systems have evolved to focus on helping to increase revenues, improve market share, or to gain a competitive advantage.

Strategic Timing. "Every morning in Africa, a gazelle wakes up. It knows it must run faster than the fastest lion or it will be killed. Every morning a lion wakes up. It knows it must outrun the slowest gazelle or it will starve to death. It doesn't matter whether you are a lion or a gazelle: when the sun comes up, you'd better be running." [13] As this analogy illustrates, the competitive advantage of any business is never a permanent one. The strategic use of automation is a constant battle to stay ahead or never fall too far behind.

Insurance companies have long recognized the role of automation in organizational strategy. Some choose to be automation leaders in the belief that it gives them cost, service or marketing advantages over competitors, at least for a while. Some choose to be "close seconds" in adopting innovations in automation technology. This practice reflects a belief that being first is a costly and sometimes risky policy. Other insurers are content to wait until technological developments are well established in the industry, perhaps in the belief that this minimizes the costs of system improvements. For example, some insurers have given extensive technical and financial assistance in the automation of their agencies. Aggressive practices in this regard often reflected the insurer's strategic goals in the development of agency representation. More simply, some insurers used automation assistance programs to strengthen their positions in carefully selected agencies that produced desirable business. In a similar way, some insurers moved faster than others in providing electronic interface facilities for their agencies. The driving force was more likely to be the attainment of marketing, growth, or other strategic objectives rather than purely technical justification.

Identifying Strategic Information Systems. [14] Over the last several years, interest in the use of information systems to gain a competitive advantage over others has continued to grow. *Strategic information systems* are systems that support or shape an organization's business strategy. Articles and books on the strategic uses of information systems in the insurance industry describe these systems as providing services to policyholders and producers. But competitive information systems can also be targeted to improving organizational efficiency through a reduction in expenses by changing the way activities are performed in a company.

Strategic information systems have three characteristics. A strategic information system significantly changes business performance as measured by one or more key indicators such as return on investment, market share, expense or loss ratio. A strategic information system plays a critical role in the implementation of the company's strategic plan. If the system contributes to meeting an insurance company's goal of increasing its share of an agency's business or an agency's goal of reducing expenses per policy, then it is strategic. Lastly, an insurance organization's information system is strategic if it changes the way it does business or the way it deals with policyholders and producers, as is the case with agency/company interface. Evaluating competitive forces and taking the customer perspective are two methods that can be used to identify strategic information systems.

Competitive Forces.[15] As Exhibit 2-3 illustrates, there are four competitive forces affecting the property and liability industry in addition to the competition for capital, employees, policyholders, and agents and brokers.

Consumers. In most insurance market segments, individual consumers want their insurance needs met at the lowest possible price rather than being sold products or services that are "best" for them or are designed around state regulatory requirements. Consumers are becoming increasingly sophisticated about both the risk management and financial aspects of insurance services and are able to choose to handle loss exposures through means other than insurance when it is appropriate to do so.

New Competitors. Insurers are facing potential or growing competition from foreign insurers, reinsurers, life insurers, as well as money-center banks, security brokers/dealers and other organizations with access to large numbers of potential customers for financial services. It is relatively easy for these firms to enter the insurance industry on any basis they choose—reinsurance, excess and surplus writers, distribution only, or purchase of existing carriers. These firms also see opportunities for improved financial returns resulting from distribution cost reductions, better management, and supplying new products to existing customers.

Technology. Another major competitive force is the technological realm. All major segments of the financial services industry are investing heavily in the development of new computer and communication capabilities. Many providers of financial services permit retail customers to control options and features via toll-free numbers, account access cards for use at automatic teller machines, and personal computers. Commercial customers typically focus on cash and financial structure management. New information capabilities, such as personal computers connected to the financial institution through a telecommunications

Exhibit 2-3
Competitive Forces at Work in the Property and Liability Industry

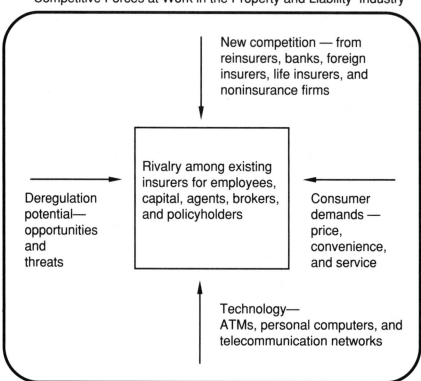

network, offer significant potential for more direct involvement of customers in controlling the delivery of services and ultimately the design of those products and services.

Deregulation. Deregulation is the fourth competitive force under consideration. The securities industry experienced significant deregulation in 1975. Banks are still undergoing extensive change as a result of it. The effect of deregulation on any industry previously protected from price competition can be a wrenching one. Cut-throat price competition by low-cost competitors threatens established companies that had become high-cost providers of service under the umbrella of regulation. Initially, competition shifts from an emphasis on service to competition based on price when an industry is deregulated.

These four major competitive forces shape the opportunities for strategies aimed at making the insurance products and services different or better in the eyes of customers, lowering costs, or finding a profitable niche. Company strategies must respond to these shifting forces.

Consumer Perspective. [16] Another way to develop strategic information systems is to concentrate on how an information system can help customers acquire policies and risk management services in better ways. Purchase and use of insurance involves several steps. The first step is to have the customer or agent determine what exposures exist. The next step is to determine the characteristics of the products needed. For example, an insurance company, agency, or risk manager could use a computer program on a personal computer to decide what coverages and limits would be most appropriate for the person, family, or business.

Once its been determined what the insurance needs are, the insurance coverage has to be purchased. The insurance companies willing to write the policies must be identified, the policies ordered, and premiums paid. Strategic information systems, such as agency/company interface and home shopping through personal computers, can be used to help agencies and insurance buyers find the insurance company willing to write the desired insurance at the most acceptable combination of coverages and price. Insurance company automated direct billing systems coupled with electronic funds transfer systems can be used to provide daily, weekly, monthly, or other customized billing plans that fit customers' cashflow needs.

Defining the Organization's Systems Architecture [17]

A systems architecture is the part of the information system's long-range plan that describes how information technology will be used to support the organization's strategic use of information systems. The first step in defining a systems architecture is to understand the factors that are critical to success in the industry as well as the high-level goals as visualized by the insurance organization's senior managers. Next the IS planner has to find out what the senior managers want done better, what competitive and operational problems cause them the most concern, and, as noted above, how systems can be used to give the company a competitive advantage with its customers. This is followed by a study of the organization's current operations and the information systems technologies that support them. This step allows the planners to develop a thorough understanding of how the company operates today. Following this analysis, the organization's long-term, marketing, service, operational, and profitability objectives are defined to set the goals to be supported by the systems architecture. Only when the business objectives have been identified is it time to identify the information technologies, how they will be used, and the migration plan for moving to the new information systems environment. Saving the technology issues for last ensures that the organization's systems architecture is driven by the organization's business strategy rather than the fads and constraints of current information systems technology.

The systems architecture describes IS management's vision of how the future business operations and strategies will be supported by information systems technology. With the appearance of more and more general management articles and books stressing the importance of using information systems strategically to achieve competitive advantage, IS managers can no longer be successful just by supporting current business activities. Gaining support for and developing a systems architecture to support an insurance organization's long-term business objectives involves the IS manager as a proactive member of senior management's development of the overall vision of the company.

Keeping up with Changing Managerial and Executive Information Requirements

The typical insurance organization experiences steady growth in the number of policies, policyholders, coverages offered, and other measures of activity. It has already been noted that information systems must expand to serve this growth. Equally important, the information system must expand to meet the needs for faster, better organized, or differently presented information. Many companies are turning to decision support systems and executive information systems to meet these needs.

Decision Support Systems. [18] Decision support systems (DSSs) are interactive systems that provide the managers with easy access to decision models and data via ad hoc queries to support the semi-structured decisions they make. Decision support systems have the following characteristics:

- They are aimed at the types of problems senior managers usually face. Managerial problems usually lack the structure needed to fully automate them and are missing some of the details needed to resolve them. Decision support systems provide the necessary level of automation so that when they are used along with human judgment, they can produce better decisions than a computer system acting alone.

- DSS combine the use of models, such as electronic spreadsheets, and analytic techniques with access to internal company databases, as well as databases external to the company to help predict outcomes for the problem being analyzed.

- Decision support systems are based on flexible and adaptable designs so they can be easily modified to support changing business and information requirements and support, as closely as possible, the decision-making approach of each user.

Executive Information Systems. [19] Executive information systems (EIS) are often confused with decision support systems. EIS are aimed at managers who currently have little or no automated support for their day-to-day responsibilities. Many executives spend very little time performing the analytical tasks associated with decision support systems. Consequently EIS are designed to provide structured reports on the status of key performance indicators. These key performance indicators measure how successful the organization is in achieving its business objectives and are determined by asking each executive using the system the following questions:

- What are the company's primary business objectives?
- What are your primary business objectives?
- What actions and processes are the most instrumental in achieving these objectives?
- What are the best indicators to track company and business unit performance in relation to those actions and processes?

Justifying Decision Support and Executive Information Systems. [20] Use of DSS and EIS seldom results in personnel and expense reductions. Since these systems evolve over time as their users define new questions to ask, or set new business objectives for the organization to meet, they do not have clearly defined completion dates. DSS and EIS are primarily designed to be flexible and easily modified rather than to provide information in a cost effective manner. Because of these reasons, DSS and EIS often appear at first glance to be difficult to cost justify. However, they can be justified by evaluating potential procedural changes such as being able to evaluate more alternatives and evaluating variances in meeting objectives; improvements in the availability of information; and the results of traditional cost/benefit analysis.

Keeping up with New Technology

The computer industry has always been blessed (or cursed, depending on your point of view) with a plethora of trade journals filled with announcements, advertisements, and articles about new information technologies such as voice recognition and response, continually improving price/performance advantages of PC over mainframes, and increased software support for distributed access to and processing of data. Although new technologies offer more options to the information system manager, this constant stream of new products demands that the manager spend a significant amount of time keeping up with the evolution of technology. Nevertheless, technological changes in the information systems environment will continue to increase each of the following: the number of users, the use of information systems, and the demand for additional information systems support.

Encouraging Innovation [21]

Information systems departments have traditionally been involved in developing new ways to reduce costs. Now, development of innovative ways to compete in the marketplace incorporates the use of information technology to a greater and greater extent. Working as a partner with user managers, IS managers can encourage innovation by educating users to think creatively about the use of technology to support their business goals. Company and IS managers can also help encourage innovation by helping them to acquire funding and providing time to develop new ideas along with the environment and encouragement necessary for budding innovators to take the plunge.

Innovation is an incremental process that involves ongoing feedback and learning from the results of each step and from overcoming obstacles that crop up from time to time. When new hardware or software is introduced, it is best to select a small, manageable, and worthwhile project for a pilot test. Installation on a pilot basis or small scale gives the individuals assigned time to learn and become comfortable with the new technologies involved. As the first and each subsequent project is successful and the technology gains acceptance as an appropriate development tool, the technology can be applied to larger projects. A supportive environment is also necessary. Unfortunately, that environment cannot be created overnight. Innovation requires a long-term management perspective to create an environment that allows taking risks with new technologies. Time is required to achieve successes, publicize the results, and demonstrate that failures will not be used as an opportunity to find fault and assign blame.

Managing Maintenance

The continual analysis, design, coding, testing, and implementation of changes to existing systems is known as maintenance. Maintenance results from regulatory changes, rate changes, changes in statistical reporting requirements, new product introduction, and hardware and software upgrades. Maintenance can as simple as correcting one rate in a personal automobile rating program or as complex as implementing a new statistical plan across all systems.

Programmers and analysts may perceive maintenance to be dull and providing few, if any, opportunities to demonstrate their creativity. However, maintenance of older systems is often very complex and requires a broad range of analytical and technical experience, skills, and knowledge. Maintenance often requires fast and accurate problem resolution. The maintenance programer might work on a simple batch reporting system one day, and a complex on-line system accesses several data bases the next. The challenge for management is to change the poor perception of maintenance as a low priority so that it will be attractive to the experienced and capable programmers maintenance activities require.

SUMMARY

Computers are located throughout the typical insurance organization. In the earliest generations of computers, they were concentrated in a "computer department" often known as the EDP department. This department is now more likely to be known by other names, including "Information Services," "Information Systems," "Management Information Systems," or the lingering "Data Processing." This department still performs production data processing, often in a central location known as the data center.

System analysts, programmers, programmer-analysts, operators, librarians, and database administrators perform major roles in the centralized information processing activities of insurance firms of size. In insurance agencies (and other small firms) these roles are performed or supervised by someone usually known as the operations manager. Hardware and software vendors are, in a sense, near-members of an organization's computer team. They provide services that enable, supplement, or substitute for activities performed by members of the IS department.

Users play an ever-increasing role in the organization's overall information processing system. They operate stand-alone PCs and terminals connected to the organization's mainframe computers. They control some of the information, some of the computer power, and have some authority over both. In a broad evolutionary process still taking place, information processing is becoming more extensively distributed throughout all but the smallest organizations. This poses new challenges in the management of information services. Through information centers and other services, the IS department helps users to meet their own needs. At the same time, those responsible for information management must integrate and coordinate information processing throughout the organization. This is no small feat given the ever-changing technology of automation.

Two aspects of information management warrant particular attention. One is the need to focus on the organization's management information system (MIS). Another focus of emerging importance is the interplay between information resources and organizational strategy. There is a current effort to focus information systems on organizational strategy and to call them strategic information systems. Clearly, in the information-intensive insurance industry, computers and the information systems that center on them are potent weapons in the battle against competitors.

Chapter Notes

1. Robert Kinderlehrer, *Handbook for Data Center Management* (Wellesley, MA: Q.E.D. Information Sciences, Inc., 1979), pp. 3-18.
2. Michael D. Gantt, "Up from Computerese," *Interface: Insurance Industry* (Winter 1978), p. 8.
3. Tom DeMarco and Timothy Lister, *Peopleware: Productive Projects and Teams* (New York, NY: Dorset House Publishing Co. Inc., 1987), pp. 150-156.
4. Barbara Canning McNurlin, ed., "Preparing for Tomorrow's Systems Jobs," *I/S Analyzer* (May 1988), pp. 5-8.
5. The Diebold Group, ed., *Automatic Data Processing Handbook* (New York, NY: McGraw-Hill, 1977), pp. 5-6.
6. Michael D. Gantt, "First Buyer: Beware of Great Expectations," *Computerworld* (29 January 1979), p. S-5.
7. National Institute for Occupational Safety and Health (NIOSH), *Potential Health Hazards of Video Display Terminals* (Cincinnati, OH: NIOSH Publication No. 81-129, 1981).
8. Richard G. Canning, ed., "Increasing Organizational Effectiveness," *EDP Analyzer* (May 1988), pp. 3-9.
9. John G. Burch, Jr. and Felix R. Strater, Jr., *Information Systems: Theory and Practice* (New York: John Wiley & Sons, 1974), pp. 30-35.
10. Burch and Strater, pp. 23-25.
11. Robert G. Murdick and Joel E. Ross, *MIS in Action* (St. Paul, MN: West Publishing Co., 1977), p. 9.
12 James L. Athearn, *Risk and Insurance* (St. Paul, MN: West Publishing Co., 1977), pp. 4-5.
13. "The Other Dimension: Technology and the City of London—A Survey," *The Economist,* July 1985, p. City of London Survey 37.
14. Richard G. Canning, ed., "Uncovering Strategic Systems," *EDP Analyzer* (October 1986), pp. 3-4.
15. Michael E. Porter, *Competitive Advantage* (New York: The Free Press, 1985), pp. 181-191.
16. Richard G. Canning, ed., "Uncovering Strategic Systems," *EDP Analyzer* (October 1986), pp. 6-7.
17. Barbara Canning McNurlin, ed., "Implementing a New Systems Architecture," *I/S Analyzer* (October 1988), pp. 6-11.
18. Sid L. Huff, "DSS Development: Promise and Practice," *Journal of Information Systems Management* (Fall 1986), p. 9.
19. David Friend, "Executive Information Systems: Successes and Failures, Insights and Misconceptions," *Journal of Information Systems Management* (Fall 1986), pp. 31-36.
20. Huff, p. 13.
21. James Brian Quinn, "Managing Innovation: Controlled Chaos," *Harvard Business Review* (May-June 1985), pp. 73-84.

CHAPTER 3

Insurance Industry Automation

Chapter 1 focused on the computer itself. Chapter 2 concentrated on the people associated with the computer. It described some of the ways in which computers have affected people and events in business, as well as ways in which people and events in business have influenced computers and their use. This discussion applied to most of American industry, including the insurance industry. Chapter 3 focuses on the use of computers in the insurance industry.

The chapter begins with a look at the need for computers in the typical insurance company. What are the unique requirements and automation objectives of an insurance company that make a large investment in computer equipment worthwhile? What can be learned from a brief review of the history of the use of computers in the insurance field? How are computers used currently?

Automation of insurance agencies is then examined. The needs of an insurance agency are quite different from those of an insurer. What are the information needs and automation objectives that make some form of agency automation an essential contributor to the future success of the agency? What are the automation options available to the agency? An overview of computers in the insurance agency touches on these and other questions.

As a matter of convenience, we will use the term *agency* to include independent and exclusive agencies as well as brokerage firms. Not every organization in the insurance industry is either an insurer or an agency. Yet insurers and agencies, together, give us the major outlines of insurance industry activity. Moreover, other organizations in the industry (regulatory or statistical organizations) are in some way associated with or deal directly with insurers or agencies. These "other" organizations will be mentioned, as their computer activities touch on those of insurers or agencies.

The last section of this chapter deals with topics of current interest to the insurance industry. Some observers believe that the insurance industry has a potential for computerization exceeded by few other segments of our economy. Specific attention will be given to the management information system (MIS) concept and its application in the insurance industry. Technological advances are expected to pave new avenues of increased automation for the industry. Such concerns as management control and privacy of information promise to present roadblocks. All things considered, there are many difficult decisions ahead as the insurance industry continues to expand the applications of computer power.

COMPUTERS IN THE INSURANCE COMPANY

An insurance company without a computer is like a cowboy without a horse: a rare sight indeed. To carry the analogy further, although the cowboy without a horse remains a cowboy, he is nonetheless at a distinct disadvantage when competing against cowboys with horses. This does not mean, of course, that every insurer has completely automated every aspect of internal processing activity. What were the earliest applications "computerized" in the insurance company? What functions are currently performed by computers?

Before describing the early computer applications in insurance companies, we should specify the need for computers and some of the objectives insurance companies have established to guide their automation strategies. In doing so, the approach taken is not unlike that of a systems analyst charged with the responsibility for determining the feasibility and the desirability of using the computer for certain functions within the company.

Why does an insurance company need a computer? This might sound like a superfluous question, but it is the basic one every systems analyst must ask. Some organizations have found themselves in a "computer mess" after jumping into computer utilization without careful consideration of this question. For a particular information application within an insurance company, the answer to this question may vary depending on the circumstances. In general, the computer can meet economically many of the information needs of an insurance company. The dynamic nature of the computer field must be kept in mind throughout this discussion. Answers that are hard to provide today may seem obvious tomorrow. For example, it is very common now for computers to rate and issue policies. It seems obvious that the actual rating of many, but of course not all, policies and their subsequent typing are chores better suited to computers than to talented people. This was not so obvious, however, a few years ago. Many underwriting and claims tasks now done manually may well be automated in the future—but it is not easy to pinpoint the tasks that will change or the order in which they will be automated.

Personal computers also illustrate this rapid change. We can easily see the need for them in the insurance organization of today, but would we have seen the need as clearly before PCs became an economic reality? In short, perception of the need for computers is affected by one's knowledge of computer capabilities.

For existing applications, the costs and benefits of automation are relatively easy to determine. The question then is, "Can the new system perform the function in a superior manner or at lower expense than the current procedure?" Although a cost-benefit analysis is not always a simple procedure, at least some cost and benefit information is available for both the existing method and the proposed method. When discussing new applications, however, the situation is different. Since the computer is performing some new function, there is no "old" method for purposes of comparison.

Existing Needs

Existing needs can be subdivided into two categories, internal and external. Internal needs arise within the insurance company itself—the needs for information processing that appear in the various departments of the insurer. External needs are the needs of those organizations outside of the insurer that require or request information processing. A computer fills an internal need when, for example, it provides up-to-date information on an automobile policy to an underwriter. It is filling an external requirement when, for example, it provides financial data to a state insurance department or to a customer.

Internal Needs.

Underwriting. The principal line underwriting functions include selection of insureds, classification and determination of proper coverage, determination of the appropriate rate or price, and producer and policyholder service. Performance of each of these functions, particularly the first two, is predicated on having the necessary information.

The application is the primary information source for the selection of insureds. A computer can be used to store this information as well as to access additional information such as motor vehicle reports. As time goes by, various changes occur to the insured and the policy. A computer is the ideal device for storing these changes and providing the underwriter with information about the insured for subsequent decisions concerning continuation or nonrenewal. This does not mean that all information necessary for the selection decision will be stored in the computer. The actual amount of information stored is a function of other considerations, including the costs and the performance of available storage facilities.

To classify and determine proper coverage also requires immediate access to information that a computer can best provide. The particular advantage of the computer is evident when any subsequent decisions must be made on a particular applicant. To be more specific, the underwriter's handling of a policy change is simplified and speeded by access to the original classification information in the computer and available to the underwriter through screen display. Renewal underwriting is also improved when the recent claim history can be compared against the overall experience of the exposure since the original policy's inception, as well as the experience of other policies the insured has with the company.

The determination of the appropriate premium can certainly be handled by the computer for many lines of business. For those lines of business that require the underwriter's judgment, the computer may generate a base quotation to be further refined by the underwriter. Also, many insurers have begun to use expert systems designed to make underwriting decisions subject to final approval by the company underwriters.

Producer and policyholder service provide many opportunities for computerization. Automation of clerical underwriting functions, such as requests for additional or missing information, not only frees underwriting staff members for other, more responsible duties, but also reduces the need for specialized underwriting expertise at every location. Once the information contained in policy files is stored in a computer file, a policy can be underwritten anywhere, not just at the servicing branch. The ability to route applications to other offices will allow the branch to concentrate on those lines and coverages making up the bulk of its business. Unusual policies can be routed to underwriters experienced in those lines and coverages in regional and/or at the home office.

Claims. The claims function of the insurer involves investigation, evaluation, negotiation, and settlement of claims in accordance with the terms of a policy. This overall function is the responsibility of the claims department. The need for computers in this area of insurer operations is intensified by the realization that claims department staff members deal directly with policyholders and thus have a great responsibility for customer relations.

Implicit in the responsibility of the claims department is the need for information. The person settling the claim will require information about the loss itself and will also require information about the specific terms of the policy. While it is true that claims adjusters usually have very specific knowledge of a given policy (for example, a homeowners policy), it is not true that every policy will have identical coverages (some have higher limits of coverage, some have broader coverages, and so on). The claims staff member, therefore, needs to know the specific coverages provided in order to determine if the loss in question is covered. The computer can fill this need for access to coverage information. In addition, computers can be used to schedule claim adjuster assignments, monitor claim and loss adjustment expenses, and estimate the cost to repair a damaged automobile. National networks allow computers to keep track of stolen and totaled cars.

The claims department also needs a computer to keep records of losses that have occurred to assist in estimating future losses, and to provide claim and loss information to actuaries and underwriters. Computers can be used to show frequency and severity of losses and to develop trends over time. The computer can, for instance, identify particular geographic areas with rising claim frequency. Today's claims departments have a vital need for accurate, up-to-date, and immediately accessible information that only computers can provide with speed and efficiency.

Accounting. Perhaps the most obvious insurance company need for computers is in the accounting department. One responsibility alone—keeping track of all money coming into and leaving the company— would be extremely difficult without a computer. It would take an army of clerks to perform the same accounting functions that computers now accomplish.

The accounting department must keep track of all premium transactions. This includes the original billing and all necessary follow-ups. It also includes premium billings for changes in coverage. Additionally, all return premiums for reduced coverage or cancellations must be processed. Historically, most of these transactions were handled through the agency. The agency billed and received premiums from the insured and periodically remitted the money to the company. Direct billing (wherein the company bills and receives the premium directly from the insured) is now common, especially in personal lines insurance. Direct billing involves even more bookkeeping work for the company accounting department and increases the need for computers.

Claims disbursements must also be recorded. How much money is being paid out in claims per month? How much money should be kept in the demand account? How many checks or drafts have been written but have not yet been cashed? These are the types of questions that computers can answer with particular advantage in support of cash management activities.

Marketing. Although agents certainly are involved in marketing, their needs are discussed in a later section. Here we are concerned with the insurer's part of the marketing effort, perhaps best described as sales management. The three major marketing functions are selecting segments of the available market, selecting the insurance services that will be most appealing to those market segments and most profitable to the company, and managing the producers who sell and service the market segments. [1]

Some types of insurance policies are more profitable to an insurance company than others. The company naturally wants to sell as many of the more profitable policy lines as possible. The tricky part is determining which policies are profitable, the geographical area in which they are profitable, and the degree of profitability. This requires the laborious accumulation, organization, and summarization of detail to which the computer is so uniquely suited. Even where this type of analysis can be performed manually, the computer offers results far more quickly.

The sales management function of an insurer can benefit from computers in managing the agency plant. There is a continuing need for timely information about each agency. What type of business has the agency been submitting? How much premium does the agency generate? What about the claim history and other aspects of the quality of the business written by the agency? Insurers normally terminate representation by agencies that fail to meet minimum standards. To go unchallenged, such terminations should be based on accurate data for the benefit of companies and agencies.

The role of the computer in the marketing area is given great attention by many insurance company executives. It is not so much that the need has been ignored in the past, but that information now stored in the computer for other purposes is being channeled to sharpen the marketing effort.

Planning. Managers of insurance companies are aware of the growing potential of computers to enhance the planning process. In particular, the computer aids the analysis of the cyclical fluctuations in underwriting results that beset the insurance industry. A computer can be helpful in corporate planning since it can be used to develop a variety of possible business scenarios. A computer model allows systematic evaluation of the effects of changes in economic and market variables on company results. Most company executives believe that use of the computer is the only way to come up with worthwhile projections.

Another need for computers in the area of planning involves the recording of goals and objectives. A project management system, in the form of computer software, allows an overall management plan to be constructed and disseminated in the most intricate detail. The computer could be programmed to identify performance dependencies within the organization. Other sophisticated management planning procedures including Critical Path Method (CPM) and Programmed Evaluation and Review Technique (PERT) are usually feasible only with a computer and the necessary software.

Control. Automation enhances the control process by improving the information used to measure unit, department, and organization performance. The computer can summarize information and generate management reports and may be programmed to highlight exceptionally good or poor results. Obviously, control reports generated by the firm's automated information system provide more timely information than would otherwise be available.

The organization's overall information system incorporates a management information system (MIS). A properly designed MIS allows executives and managers to monitor the important activities throughout the organization. They will not have to wait until some periodic review process to determine how well lower level managers have met their objectives. The MIS, if properly constructed, will incorporate all existing systems, "observe" the ongoing performance of these subordinate systems, and report conditions that exceed predetermined tolerance.

External Needs.

Policyholders. The insurance company has an obvious need for computers in dealing with policyholders. This does not mean that computers should replace human contact. On the contrary, there seems to be little enough human contact already. But the insurer needs to provide the insured with a considerable amount of information. First of all, the insured must receive a policy from the company. A computer can prepare policies more quickly, more accurately, and at lower cost than typists can.

Direct billing would be economically impossible without the computer. The computer's role will continue to grow with the emerging choices available for payment plans.

Another computer need arises from consumerism and government regulation. Regulators require that insurers provide their policyholders with detailed information, such as information on coverage options available.

If not required now, legislative proposals may soon require companies to show the various deductibles available and the resultant changes to the premium. This may, in some cases, require rating the policy a number of times to arrive at multiple premium figures.

Agencies. The specific needs of agencies are a separate topic to be covered later, but the insurer's needs with regard to agencies may be examined here. The insurer needs to provide a wealth of information to the agency, such as premium and loss figures. These figures will be even more helpful to the agency if they are organized by geographic area, type of policy, and other categories. Reports of this nature are reviewed with interest, since they show how well the agent is doing from the company's point of view. Agents are eager to provide the insurer with profitable business. Most agents are also eager to receive information from insurers on the status of outstanding claims. This includes information about the amount of the reserve established by the insurer and the exact amount of any partial or advance payment. It is important for agency staff members to know of all transactions between the insurance company and the agent's customers. Without timely reporting by insurers, agents lose the ability to speak knowledgeably to the policyholder.

Another demand being placed on insurers is the expansion of electronic interface with their agencies. Interface is seen as a way to lower the cost of distribution by eliminating the duplicate processing of information in the agency and company. Interface is also viewed as the means of giving agents fast access to the claim and policy information contained in company computer files.

Associations and Bureaus. The bureaus and agencies that collect statistics from insurers and analyze and report the result would find it almost impossible to perform their tasks without computers. How did they survive before the age of the computer? In general, they did not collect as much information from member companies. Statistics were kept on very broad coverage categories. The demand today is for more detailed statistics.

For example, until several years ago products liability coverage was not reported as a separate coverage by statistical organizations, but was combined with other liability coverages. When products liability claims skyrocketed and coverage became very expensive, insurance regulators demanded specific premium and loss figures for products liability coverage alone.

Does the statistical organization need a computer because it must keep more information? Or does the statistical organization keep more information because it has a computer? There is no satisfactory, clear-cut answer to this question. But the question helps keep the information-gathering function in perspective. The need for computers in the statistical area is not simply to gather more and more information, but also to manage more effectively and economically the information already being collected.

In addition to statistical and rating organizations, there are other associations, organizations, or situations that influence the need for information management. An example is a reinsurance pool of companies. The primary insurer will report certain statistical data to the pool. These reports are somewhat standard, requiring information already available in most companies. At other times the request will require a specific search or tally. In such cases, a computer eases the burden.

Regulators. The insurance company must cope with the ever increasing information needs of those charged with regulating the insurance industry. For instance, in recent years regulators have established pinpointed reporting requirements to facilitate "early warning" of threats to insurer solvency. As with most government activity, the trend is toward more rather than less.

Regulators, in turn, are under increasing pressure from the insurance buying public. Representatives of the public, especially consumer advocates, have become more sophisticated in their requests for insurance data. Furthermore, annual reports themselves have increased significantly in size and scope over the last ten years.

An insurance company cannot satisfy information demands with simple premium and loss totals. Insurers are required to provide data by geographical areas, type of business, and even specific coverages within policies. The variations of statistical analysis are practically endless. The primary value of the computer in this context is its ability to arrange, reclassify, sort, summarize, and reproduce the data stored within it and to do these things accurately, speedily, and economically.

To meet their information requirements, the National Association of Insurance Commissioners (NAIC) has created the State Computing Network. This network is the electronic link between all state insurance departments and the insurance database housed at the NAIC's administrative office. The system allows regulators overnight electronic access to customized reports of property and liability insurers' financial data on a state-by-state basis. Reports produced include lists of leading writers of a certain line of business, calculations of guaranty fund assessments, and loss ratios by company, line, and state.

Objectives of Insurance Company Automation [2]

Traditional Objectives. The traditional objectives of data processing have tended to focus on cost and staff reductions, handling large volumes of paperwork resulting from the growth of the company, increased requirements for data from external sources such as rating bureaus and state regulators, and the demand for more information by insurance company managers and executives.

Cost Reduction or Displacement. Automation has always been an attractive way to replace rising labor costs with hardware costs, which are going down, by automating the most repetitive and routine tasks. To the extent that the insurance industry has had repetitive tasks to automate, it has automated them successfully. Another aspect of this objective has been to improve the productivity of the insurance industry's employees and proportionately reduce the expenses associated with delivery and administration of the industry's products.

Processing Voluminous Amounts of Data. Automation has traditionally provided insurers with an economical way to handle the large volumes of data that they must process. The processing of policies and claims involves millions of pieces of data. Policy processing includes the functions of risk selection, premium calculation, policy issuance, data entry, statistical reporting, and policy maintenance. Each policy generates an unpredictable number of transactions, including quotations, bills, renewals, endorsements, cancellations, and reinstatements. The life cycle of a claim includes claims reporting, coverage verification, inspection, adjustment, settlement, one or more payments, and subsequent follow-up reporting. The problem of handling this large volume of data is compounded by the number of times it is handled. The data an agent collects might be handled later by an underwriter, rater, loss control technician, policy typist, premium auditor, and billing clerk and then handled all over again when there is an endorsement.

Better Decision Making. Among the critical judgments made in insurance companies are those that deal with product design, customer interaction, information gathering and analysis, risk evaluation and transfer analysis, loss reserve estimation, and loss adjustment. These judgments require specialized information rather than masses of data. As noted in Chapter 2, for information to be useful it must be accurate (free of human errors), timely, complete (providing all of the information the user needs and no more), concise (on-line tables and graphs rather than mounds of data), and relevant (provide need-to-know rather than nice-to-know information). Automation is invaluable in aiding management decisions when used to select items worthy of managerial attention and when used to estimate the consequences of actions being considered.

Objectives of Emerging Importance.

Create a Competitive Advantage. In many insurance companies, top management historically looked on data processing primarily as a support function for performing routine accounting operations. In these companies, the computer was not seen as a tool for increasing revenues or improving market share. Insurers now look to information systems as a way of creating a competitive advantage by giving them new ways to strengthen relationships with their employees, agencies, brokerage firms, reinsurers, and other groups that play major roles in the firm's success. These groups are called *strategic stakeholders*. Information systems can be used to create innovative incentives to attract and sustain contributions from strategic stakeholders in a number of ways, some of which are shown in Exhibit 3-1. The approaches with each strategy may or may not be mutually exclusive. For example, producing more efficiently would give an insurer the option of increasing dividends to its owners, lowering the price of its products, increasing its employee and producer compensation, or a combination of two or more of these. The key to an insurer's creation of a competitive advantage with its strategic stakeholders is its ability to identify and provide the necessary incentives to meet the stakeholder's various and often divergent needs in an innovative and competitive manner.

Optimal Use of Information Resources. [3] Technology has already permitted insurers to reap the easy benefits of automation. With most of the big labor saving applications already in place, insurers have moved to applications in which gains are less quantifiable. To evaluate these systems and allocate funds for their development, top management must know the true costs of the company's investment, understand the organizational consequences of the new systems, and be able to measure the benefits. These factors are discussed below.

Reduce Total Costs. Proposals for new systems or system upgrades may concentrate on the technical costs of the system but ignore the people costs and how the projected benefits will be achieved. These overlooked costs include initial training plus on-the-job training cost—cost of the trainees, trainers, and the training facilities. Startup costs are also often overlooked. Startup costs include lower productivity during the initial learning phase, job interruptions caused by new and unfamiliar procedures, time spent in meetings to discuss new ways of handling work, and management time spent handling morale problems that crop up. Poorly conceived and implemented systems only compound the effect of these costs.

Exhibit 3-1
Strategic Stakeholder Incentives That Can Be Created Through Automation

STRATEGY / STAKEHOLDERS	INVESTORS	EMPLOYEES	AGENTS & BROKERS	POLICYHOLDERS
PRODUCE MORE EFFICIENTLY	• Increase profits	• Better salaries	• Higher commissions or bonuses	• Lower prices
CREATE NEW INDUCEMENTS		• Automate routine tasks to enrich jobs	• Computer-assisted underwriting authority	• Ability to create own insurance programs & risk management reports
CREATE ENTRANCE INCENTIVES AND EXIT BARRIERS	• Automated marketing support for agents of parent life subsidiary		• Improved services • Competitive prices • Lower operating expenses	
REDISTRIBUTE INDUCEMENTS		• Decentralize authority and responsibility, tying compensation to results		
INFLUENCE PERCEPTIONS OF VALUE	• Technological leadership	• Technological leadership	• Technological leadership • Flexibility	• Technological leadership • Flexibility • Convenience
CHANGE STAKEHOLDERS		• Broader skilled	• Deal directly with insurance buyers	
CHANGE STAKEHOLDER POWER			• Tie agent/broker closer to company	

Achieve Organizational Objectives. One of the traditional objectives of automation has always been to improve the way the company operates. A more recent objective of automation is to improve customer satisfaction by providing faster, more accurate information. However, both of these can be accomplished only by transforming the functions and tasks of employees, not by simply speeding up the work. Optimum use of the organization's information resources requires integration with strategic plans that show how the company should evolve to achieve its business objectives. It is especially true of insurance firms that automation and strategy are dovetailed; that is, automation can no longer be considered a mere means to the organization's objectives. Instead, the level of automation for internal processing and the extent of agency interface are major components of an insurer's strategy. Automated processing and delivery are built-in parts of new insurance products and govern their pricing and viability. An insurance company's information system helps define the company; investment in the information system is an essential part of its strategy to shape its future.

Meet Stakeholder Needs. Management needs techniques for measuring the effects of new systems to ensure that information resources are being used most profitably. Traditional methods look at individual tasks to determine if each one is made more efficient. Future automation systems will be judged by the satisfaction of the insurer's *strategic stakeholders.* Stakeholders are those groups that have a clearly recognizable interest in the success of the organization, including employees, investors and owners, customers, suppliers, and those who sell the firm's products. Is the benefit of the system to the stakeholder greater than the contribution it makes to the insurer? Is the contribution greater than the cost of inducing the stakeholder to make it? Existing systems must also be measured periodically against the insurer's business objectives to determine if they are truly helping the insurer, rather than simply assuming that they are as essential as the day they were implemented.

Evolution of Insurance Company Automation

One of the first computer applications within insurance companies was accounting for premiums and losses. These accounting systems were, and still are, often referred to as *functional systems,* since each system performed one function. That is, a premium system was designed to perform all premium processing, and a loss system was designed to perform all loss processing. The programs for the premium system were entirely separate from those of the loss system. These systems were transaction oriented. That is to say, they were designed around the basic premium transactions of the insurance company. In contrast, most of the systems being developed today are oriented around the policy. The amount of data collected by these first systems was scanty by today's standards. Because of their transaction orientation, these early loss and premium systems were incompatible in nature. A premium transaction has a different nature and timing than a loss transaction. Every policy has at least one premium transaction. This is not the case with loss transactions. Current systems resolve this disparity by combining the two functions (not systems) in one overall system that contains all of the data concerning each policy rather than a series of sequential transactions.

After functional systems, insurance company data processing departments typically turned their attention to the automatic rating of policies. Personal lines, specifically private passenger automobile policies, were the first applications. Typically, systems were developed to rate and print personal automobile insurance policies by companies that had large volumes of business in this line. Concurrent with the development of rating systems, many companies developed direct billing systems that required the insured to remit the premium payment directly to the insurance company. This allowed the company to take advantage of the computer's efficiency in handling payments. It also provided the opportunity for earlier receipt (and use) of premium dollars. Prior to this time, the majority of premium payments were collected by the agent and then submitted in total to the company once a month.

As computer policy rating gained popularity, attention turned to the automation of underwriting functions. These early underwriting automation attempts were based on the idea of assigning point values to specific factors pertinent to the loss exposure. In the case of an automobile policy, for example, points would be assigned for traffic citations received by the insureds. Rather than automatically rejecting applications when the total number of points reached some predetermined figure, most computer programs were designed to refer the applications with high point totals to an underwriter who reviewed them before making a decision.

Since these early point systems, automated systems have gradually taken on more and more of the duties of the underwriter. In a sense, modern systems developed using expert systems technology guide the underwriter through the analysis of an application and make the decisions unless the underwriter intervenes. Even with such contemporary expert system technology, many observers believe that computer underwriting works best as an aid to the underwriter rather than as a replacement for the underwriter. The time-consuming process of gathering information from various company databases and preliminary analysis are transferred to the expert underwriting system. The underwriter is left to perform the crucial function that requires more than a computer program: the decision as to whether to commit the insurer's capital to a new exposure.

Within the next ten years many of the large insurers will use computers as the underwriting and policy production unit for the majority of personal lines and simpler commercial lines policies. Their major objective is to reduce or stabilize long-run operating costs and losses by applying underwriting standards consistently against all policy applications.

Current Developments

The spread of automation within insurance companies continues: the process is not over yet. More and more lines of business are becoming computer-rated and computer-issued, although this usually takes place within the context of the on-line, policy-oriented systems mentioned earlier. Other functions being automated include ceded reinsurance administration, electronic publishing of policy documents and forms, and specialized functions such as investment accounting and legal research. These are functions that have little direct association with policies or policy transactions. Insurance companies are often at the leading edge of advances in applications of computer technology. The future will be considered later in this chapter.

COMPUTERS IN THE INSURANCE AGENCY

Insurance agencies and brokerage firms of all sizes rely increasingly on automated products and services to support daily operations. The proliferation of software for microcomputers places automation within the grasp of the smallest agency.

The use of computers in agencies has been and will continue to be unique. The agency's relationship with the insurer is at the center of this uniqueness. In the case of independent agencies, multiple companies complicate that relationship. While independent in one sense, the agency is also interdependent with the companies for which it is in the legal position of agent. Like agencies, insurance brokerage organizations require close, accurate, and almost constant contact with insurance companies. There are important distinctions between a brokerage and an agency, but their automation needs are similar. In the discussion that follows, they are both covered by the term agency.

Though there are various kinds of agents and brokers, throughout the following discussion agencies will be assumed to be independent businesses representing more than one company. This approach is used for two reasons. First, concepts described for use in a multiple company environment can be modified to apply to a single company environment fairly easily. To do the reverse is not so easy. Second, the area of multiple company relationships provides the greatest challenge to computerization and is receiving the greatest attention.

Information Needs

All agencies perform most of all the functions described below to some extent. However, the priorities assigned to these functions will differ from agency to agency. In addition, as an agency's business environment changes over time with the addition of new customers, sales programs, and through mergers or acquisitions, functions with a low priority today may become extremely important in the future.

Prospect Information. Prospect information is important to the overall agency sales effort. Information that is well organized and up-to-date can increase sales productivity considerably. In many cases the information required for a personal account is different from the information required for a commercial account. Information needed for a personal account prospect includes date of birth, number of dependents, spouse/marital data, occupation, and social security number. A commercial account prospect, on the other hand, requires legal entity, officers/titles, contracts, location information, fiscal year, nature of the business, and special industry codes. It is important to be able to page through this information quickly to review or update remarks and call histories.

Sales Management Information. The sales management function includes several sales support tasks. Marketing strategies are molded by the mission and unique characteristics of each agency. They should reflect in-depth knowledge about present and potential customers. Detailed information is required to monitor sales activities and provide sales management reports. It is also necessary to control the various sales activities by producing follow-up reports and sales statistics to compare actual results with the agency's goals and the results of prior years. Sales productivity is also a key management consideration. Information should be available for producers regarding the disposition of sales calls, success ratios, premium/commission volume, and so on.

Sales analysis touches on one of the key issues in agency management today. Some observers contend that agents cannot or do not devote enough of their time to selling and servicing insurance products. It is argued that so much time is spent on the paperwork and internal tasks of the agency that too little time is left for selling and service functions. As the computer reduces the need for human labor in the agency, the agent should have more time for selling and service.

Client Information. Client information originates with the sale of a policy. It serves as the core of the agency's database since most of the transactions processed in the agency contain client information. An automated client information file is essentially an electronic client file cabinet that provides a single service for all inquiries about a client. If a producer or customer service representative needs client information, there should be no need to pull a physical file. All pertinent information should be displayed on a computer screen with the option to print the information on paper as needed. In addition to the detailed information about a client, agencies need data about the client's policies, claims, accounts receivable balance, and other details. A client information file gives the agencies' marketing staff ability to ensure that all coverage needs have been addressed.

Agencies also need client information to identify problem clients such as those who routinely pay late, request numerous endorsements to small premium policies, or do not follow risk reduction recommendations. Separating problem accounts from good accounts allows the agency to focus marketing activities on the good clients through more frequent contacts and better service.

Rating. The rating function supports the process of issuing quotations and proposals for new business, policy changes, and renewals. Agencies need the capability to issue quotations in a timely manner for all major lines of business in support of the sales effort. If the agency is fully automated, it is important that the quotation process be completely integrated into its main computer system and not require the re-entry of information already in the system. For example, name, address, and location information should be obtained from the system's database. Unfortunately, agency rating systems may exist on stand-alone microcomputers rather than as parts of the agency's computer system. The agency needs the ability to prepare multiple quotations for the same application using different companies, limits, coverages, and so on, without duplicating any information.

Policy Activity Processing. The agency must process new business, policy changes, and renewals with a minimum of file pulling and duplication of information. In addition the agency should be able to issue binders and print policy documents and certificates of insurance primarily from the data already in the agency's system.

Claim Processing. Claim processing is a very important customer service, and the agency requires comprehensive claim processing functions, including an effective inquiry system, ACORD claim reports, claim histories, and status monitoring. It is important for the agency to have the ability to monitor the status of a claim until it is closed by the company. Management reports are required for control purposes. Claims management information fosters good service to clients and improves agency/company communications. Claims information may be used for marketing purposes, profitability analysis, contingency agreements, and monitoring company service (e.g., average time to close).

Word Processing. Most agency correspondence with prospects, clients, and companies involves the use of form letters or modified form letters that are stored in the system. Since considerable repetition is involved in policy processing, the agency should not be required to re-create letters, memos, and confirmations for every transaction. The word processing system should maintain a file of frequent documents that can be accessed and modified for a specific transaction as required. The agency also requires the facility to create and maintain special documents, such as proposals and risk surveys that usually require multiple revisions. The word processing system should also be capable of inserting data automatically from the agency's database into a predefined form letter.

Accounting. Premium accounting and general accounting are important functions within the agency's operation. The accounting system should support all new business, endorsements, renewal, and audit transactions. Since bookkeeping is often centralized within the agency operation, proper security measures are required for specific activities. For example, producers and customer service representatives require access to accounting information during the course of the business day (e.g., outstanding balances and status of accounts), but they may not need access to general ledger financial reports and summaries.

Agencies require a complete general ledger system for the production of financial reports. These reports serve as the basis of management control. An accounts receivable system is also required to control invoicing and cash receipts on both an *open item* and *balance forward* basis. The open item by invoice method permits the agency to carry forward all accounting details for each transaction. The balance forward by account method only provides a total amount for months other than the current month. Agencies must also have the capability to monitor all direct bill transactions and to reconcile company statements— *accounts current* system for controlling payments to companies and an *accounts payable* system. An automated checkwriting capability with automatic posting to general ledger accounts may also be required by large agencies. All accounting functions should be integrated with the management information system.

Agency/Company Interface. Agencies use both *batch store-and-forward* and *interactive* interface. With batch store-and-forward interface, the agency enters the day's applications, policy changes, and other transactions into the agency's system and instructs the system to transmit these transactions to the desired company. With interactive interface, a two-way "conversation" takes place between a person in the agent's office and the computer in the company's office. Interactive interface requires the hands-on involvement of an agency employee during the transmission.

In the event that specific types of transactions cannot be transmitted electronically or if the company involved does not interface with the agency, the agency's system should print an application on paper for mailing to the company.

As agency/company interface broadens, many benefits should accrue to the insurance industry and ultimately to policyholders, the most important of which should be better service and improved insurance products. Freed of some data processing and communications chores, the agent should be able to concentrate on client needs, such as more detailed surveys and more comprehensive analysis for clients. These surveys and analyses could produce suggestions for better coverages, strengthened safety precautions, and application of an array of risk management techniques. This might lead to lower premiums for some clients and better underwriting experience for the agency. The hope is that agency/company interface will remove much of the nonselling burden from the agent, thus allowing more time for the agent's managerial and professional work.

Objectives of Agency Automation

The informational and operational needs of an insurance agency were discussed above. Agencies have automated to meet these needs and to achieve the general advantages of office automation, including cost reductions, more timely information, and error reduction. In addition to these general benefits, agencies have focused automation efforts on the following:

Improved Profitability. Automated agencies have been found to have profit margins higher than those of agencies with manual record-keeping systems. One of the main effects of automation is the reduction in labor cost as a percentage of total revenue. Profitability can also be improved by maximizing cash flow and revenue from investment income from the short-term investment of client premiums prior to their submission to the insurer.

Improved Office Effectiveness. Agency office procedures are affected in several ways by automation. In-house agency systems permit office staff members to move away from routine tasks such as typing and filing to more productive tasks that will improve customer service. Automation also helps standardize office procedures such as those related to maintaining diaries and suspense entries to improve follow-up activities and avoid *errors and omissions* claims.

Improved Marketing. Automation significantly improves marketing effectiveness through selective identification and segmentation of clients and prospects based on the content of data stored in the computer. For example, an agency may target a specific industry. The agency computer can be used to identify all prospects in the industry that meet certain criteria such as revenue, number of employees, and location.

Current Status of Agency Automation

The vendors of computer hardware, software, and systems have shown great interest in the potential market offered by insurance agencies. Their efforts have been fruitful. It is hard to imagine an agency too small to afford and benefit from having a computer.

Agencies, like the companies they represent, face a highly competitive market. Combined with changes in the economy, competition has helped to change agencies from organizations that emphasized new business through referrals into businesses which are more completely marketing oriented. The desire to intensify marketing efforts has become a prime force in the decision to automate and in the selection and use of a system.

Automation Is a Business Issue. Automation is now a business issue, not a technical one. Specifying system requirements and identifying the resources to meet the agency's business objectives is a management function, and best handled by individuals with insurance and operational knowledge—not data processing knowledge. Agencies must make their automation decisions based on their organizations' particular needs and objectives.

Modes of Processing. Agencies use three modes of computerized processing: service bureau by mail, service bureau by terminal, and in-agency computer systems.[4] A description of these three modes and insurer agency automation assistance programs will survey the current state of computer activities within insurance agencies.

Service Bureau by Mail. Processing data by sending it to a service bureau remains a common and successful approach. In fact, many agencies that now have in-house agency automation systems started as customers of a service bureau. The service bureau by mail approach works as follows. The agency sends copies of agency cash receipts, checks, invoices, and other data entry forms for journal entries, changes to client name/address, and changes to employee data to the bureau. The data are mailed or sent by other means to the bureau at least once per month and often once a week. When they are received by the service bureau, bureau staff members key-enter the agency information, process it on the bureau's computer, and produce various monthly financial and management reports including the income statement, balance sheet, aged receivables report, client statements, and ledger cards. After the processing cycle has been completed, the bureau returns the computer output to the agency by mail or other delivery arrangements. This processing arrangement is sometimes called "batch service bureau" processing.

Advantages of *service bureau by mail* processing include small capital investment, no site preparation, limited special training, minimal agency software requirements, fast conversion, and no long-term commitment. The normally small capital investment required to begin batch processing is one of the most important advantages. Because of the small investment, many agents follow this approach for their first entry into computerization. If it proves successful, and it often does, the agency is likely to stay with service bureau processing. There is no reason to convert to some other mode of processing if the system meets the agency's objectives and is cost effective.

A batch processing arrangement with a service bureau requires no site preparation within the agency since the computer is located at the service bureau. This benefit is particularly important to the many agents who have little office space. The other modes of processing usually require setting aside some significant space.

Little training is required for agency employees to make use of this processing service—a significant cost saver. Since the procedures are easily learned, the agency is not in the risky position of relying on one or more highly trained employees. Since batch system procedures can normally be learned in a short period of time, employees seldom have to leave the agency for training.

Since batch processing by a service bureau is usually limited to the most common management functions of the agency, requirements for specialized software are minimal. When special software is required, the service bureau is usually available to write the program for a fee.

Manual procedures can usually be converted quickly to a service bureau batch processing system. Unlike the terminal and computer approaches, mail-in processing usually allows for simple and fast conversion of existing bookkeeping and accounting data to the computer system. The service bureau provides on-site instructions and helps implement the conversion. It should be noted that some terminal and minicomputer systems now place high emphasis on ease of conversion.

Perhaps the most significant aspect of service bureau batch processing within agencies is that it seldom demands any long-term commitment. This is especially important to the insurance agency that faces a lack of consensus on the best way to reach computer compatibility with the companies represented. Some agencies remain with batch processing while waiting for clarifications of the interface picture.

Service Bureau by Online Terminal Processing. Although normally more expensive than batch processing, online terminals offer a relatively low-cost entry into computer processing. A terminal or personal computer with communication capabilities is normally placed in the agency by a service bureau on a monthly rental basis. Whenever the agency wants to use one of the service bureau functions, a telephone call is made from the agency to the service bureau to connect the terminal or PC to the service bureau's computer.

Many agencies have acquired an online terminal to take advantage of the many data processing applications available. For instance, premium finance contract processing can be added to the online service. With enough additional features, many agents are able to cost-justify the online service.

A key advantage of online terminals over mail-in batch processing is the potential for reduction of errors. Service bureaus have attained a reputation for high accuracy in processing, but overall accuracy is hampered by the sequence of activities needed to correct an error. Under a batch system, entries are coded onto special forms which are, of course, gathered together and then forwarded to the service bureau. If any errors are detected, they will be returned to the agency for correction. Errors must then be corrected by the agency and returned to the service bureau. This can be a time-consuming process. It also leads to additional complications since accounts are not completely accurate and up-to-date. (A client may be sent a past due notice for a bill that has already been paid.) The online terminal can improve overall accuracy and timeliness since corrections are made in the agency. If a policy number is entered into the system and found to be incorrect for each company the agency represents, the bureau is notified immediately. Under a batch system, notification might take several days, a week, or even longer. With an online terminal the major responsibility for errors in data going into the system rests with the agency.

The fast service afforded by online terminals is significant to the insurance agency. Rather than waiting for the mail or some delivery service, the agency can, with an online terminal and attached printer, receive reports directly and immediately. Once the books of the agency have been closed, monthly processing can begin. The response time for monthly reports can be reduced from several days to several hours.

There is usually no long-term commitment associated with online terminals. Since the terminals can be rented from the service bureau, cancellation is not a momentous decision. Service bureaus usually retain the right to the software. Because of their proprietary interest in the programs and because the programs have little custom-tailoring, service bureaus provide online service without a long-term agreement.

With an online terminal, the agency has immediate access to the data stored in the computer. Under the batch by mail system, data available in the agency was only as current as the last report received, perhaps a month earlier. Online processing makes all data resident in the service bureau's computer available for display to the terminal user. It is important to note that data is not automatically available in the exact format the agency might desire. Programs have to be written that will allow the user to access the desired information via the terminal. In most cases, the necessary software is already available, but it is wise for the agency to ascertain the exact nature of the data stored and the formats in which this data may be retrieved.

Much more than with batch processing, online terminal processing positions the agency closer to direct communications with the companies it represents. Once employees have been trained to operate the terminal, little additional training will be required to operate a company terminal when placed in the agency. Similarly, online terminal processing helps prepare employees for an in-agency computer system.

Standalone In-Agency System (Agency Management System). For the agency that has a growing level of paper work and, therefore, a growing need for the benefits of computerization, the purchase, rental, or lease of a computer is inevitable. A number of vendors offer full-function minicomputer and microcomputer systems with application software specifically designed to meet agency information processing needs. Most of these vendors provide training in the use of the system, assistance in conversion to the new system, and service after the installation in the form of on-site support and toll-free support over the telephone. These systems are usually purchased as complete, ready-to-use systems rather than as highly customized or unique systems. They are often referred to as *agency management systems* (AMS). Other names are *general purpose system* and *full-function system.* More casually, agency employees are likely to say "the computer" and refer to other computer systems in the agency by their particular function, such as a (standalone) rating computer.

Advantages of an Agency Management System. Although expensive, the agency's own computer offers some direct advantages over service bureau processing. These include data storage within the agency, greater control over data, greater control over costs, the ability to expand with agency growth, and direct communication linkage with other organizations when available. For most agencies, the issue is not whether but when to acquire an in-agency computer. The capabilities and available benefits continue to grow dramatically. It is difficult to speak of the cost side while hardware and software continue to achieve marked improvements. Nonetheless, you can picture agency computerization as generally declining in cost. That is, a given data processing task (for example, maintaining policyholder files for 1,000 insureds) is probably done at lower cost today than it was three years ago. Similarly, the price tag for an additional computer or terminal work station is likely to be lower than it was three years ago. Furthermore, the mushrooming capabilities of microcomputers means that only large agencies require minicomputer-based systems. In sum, for most agencies, the future is likely to include a computer as vendors achieve economies of high volume, as they compete to enhance system capabilities without corresponding increases in prices, and as they migrate all or parts of their mini-based systems to microcomputers.

Data Stored Within the Agency. Having the agency data stored on the premises offers a psychological benefit. With direct control of data and of the computer, the agency has greater opportunity to "control its own destiny." This can be an important item in the agency's computerization timetable. There are major and minor frustrations inevitably present in the service bureau relationship—waiting for service is a common example. The agent cannot expect the bureau to drop everything else and work on a special request. If a minicomputer and programmer were available in the agency, an agency manager could indeed ask the programmer to stop everything else and meet the special request. This is an expensive luxury, and most agencies prefer to employ a vendor's software without modification. Agencies can exercise a measure of control over the service provided by a vendor's system by adding optional features and upgrades and by expanding the number of workstations in the system.

Greater Control Over Data. The second advantage is closely related to the first. The in-agency computer offers to the agency the specific advantage of having control of the data in the computer. This means that the agency is not limited in the use of that data to the routine reports and other standard output produced by the service bureau. The agency can add other systems or subsystems to those already run by the computer if it is willing to assume control over the system. Having control of the data also enables the agency to modify reports and other parts of the software to better meet a particular need.

Greater Control Over Costs. The agency also gains the benefits of being able to spread a growing volume of transactions over a fixed equipment cost. Under most batch and online terminal processing, at least part of the monthly fee is based on transaction volume. Therefore, as business increases, processing costs increase. Some allowance is usually made for economies of scale achieved by the vendor. Still, the benefits of agency growth seem to be shared, at least in part, with the vendor.

Expandability. The in-agency computer also offers the ability to expand as the agency grows. As the needs of the agency increase, additional peripheral equipment can be purchased to upgrade the overall capacity of the computer. With a service bureau, the agency may find, after a period of time, that more functions are needed than the particular bureau can provide. The agency may even find it necessary to change service bureaus to obtain additional functions. Having an agency management system leaves the agency free to improve, downgrade, or otherwise modify the hardware system. Above all, this leads to a computer system that can be tailored to agency needs through expenditures that are under agency control.

Interface Capability. Having an in-agency computer system positions the agency nearer to achievement of ideal interface with insurers and other organizations. Agencies can interface with insurers through terminals used for that purpose. This *company terminal interface* is considered inferior to interface between the agency's AMS and the insurer's computer system. It is considered inferior because all data entered through the terminal must be re-entered in the AMS. From the agency standpoint, interface is far from ideal if data must be entered twice. (The subject of agency/company interface is discussed at length below.)

The Drive Toward an Integrated System. The microcomputer revolution brought pronounced changes in agency automation. At the beginning of the 1980s, the dominant agency systems were minicomputer-based. They succeeded in integrating most of the information processing needs of the agency. They maintained policyholder records, performed financial accounting, created management reports, and did a great many other data processing tasks with near-perfect integration. There emerged the image of an agency system that did it all and did it all at once. That ideal was ever elusive but remarkably persistent. The microcomputer explosion brought an end to the myth of the single system. Instead of a total system, the new look of the automated agency is that of a number of computers. In addition to its major computer (mini or micro) with a number of terminals, the typical agency might have one or more micros dedicated to specific tasks or functions such as for a specialty line unit or a telemarketing unit. The current quest is for ways to integrate the AMS and the standalone computer systems that proliferated in the 1980s.

Agency Automation Assistance Programs

The late 1970s and early 1980s saw automation sweep through the ranks of insurance agencies. Many large- and medium-sized agencies obtained computer systems. Typically, these systems were complete hardware/software packages acquired from vendors. The impetus came from agents themselves and from enterprising vendors. At least at the start, insurance companies watched from a distance and rarely played a direct role in the automation of the agency force.

This picture changed drastically as insurance companies became deeply involved in the process of automating insurance agencies. It was not surprising that the direct writing and exclusive agency companies oversaw the automation of their agents. The more notable turn of events was a rush of insurers into direct involvement in the automation of independent agents. Insurers changed from onlookers to committed players. They competed vigorously against one another in offering assistance for agency automation and interface connections—so vigorously, in fact, that the activity could be described as a race to place automation equipment in exchange for premium commitments. Their motivation was not simply the desire to develop efficient data exchange interface. Equally important to most insurers was the desire to strengthen (or protect) relationships with key agencies, which usually meant the insurers' larger agencies.

Some insurers became, in effect, vendors of computer systems to agencies. Some insurers purchased system vendors and others joined consortiums to achieve the same result. Some offered insurers extensive technical help and some offered generous financial assistance to selected agencies to aid their automation.

The automation financing programs offered by insurers usually provided agents with an agency automation system in return for a production commitment. The commitment was usually expressed in terms of the number of dollars of premium for each dollar of the system's cost, or on specified premium production goals or policies in force. The danger of these programs was the potential for development of strained relationships between the insurers and their agencies if the agency was unable to meet production goals because of the insurer's uncompetitive products, pricing, or service.

Insurers have advanced a number of qualitative reasons for acquiring an ownership interest in one or more agency automation vendors. These insurers had an automated system they could recommend with confidence to agencies. Vendors gained access to new technological developments and funding. From an agent's perspective, vendor ownership by insurers provided the financial stability and capitalization needed to support continued enhancements, problem resolution, and development of interface capabilities.

Other insurers have deliberately avoided ownership of automation vendors. In designing agency automation financing programs and developing agency/company interface, these insurers believe they must avoid becoming "locked-in" to one vendor in a way that might exclude some of their agents. They emphasized the idea that there was no system available that could meet the automation needs of every agent. These insurers did not believe consortiums could provide them a satisfactory return on investment. They were also concerned about the vendor's ability to maintain the software in a fast-changing technological world. Rather than take an equity position in a vendor, these insurers chose to direct more of their expenditures toward automating their internal operations to hasten and expand interface.

AGENCY/COMPANY INTERFACE

Agency/Company interface has been defined by ACORD as the replacement of some portion of existing mail and telephone communications among agents and companies with two-way electronic communications directly between an agency computer system and multiple insurance company computers directly or through a network. The electronically communicated data must be edited and ready for direct processing by the receiver's computer upon receipt.

Advantages

Agency/company interface has received extensive attention because it holds the promise of a number of advantages. Agency/company interface is expected to:

- Reduce the number of data entry errors and missing pieces of policy and client information
- Reduce duplication of effort by agency and company personnel;
- Reduce the cost of product delivery for both the agencies and insurance companies
- Improve communications and working relationships among agencies and insurers
- Improve service to the insurance consumer
- Improve the competitive position of the agencies and companies that have interface

Types of Interface

Interactive Interface. *Interactive interface* is a communication method in which a "dumb" terminal (terminal without intelligence provided by a CPU or microchip processor), personal computer, or terminal connected to the agency's automation system is connected to an insurance company's computer. This connection can be a direct connection between the agency and company, or a dial-up connection direct to the company or through a communication network. When interactive interface is used, an agency employee is prompted by the insurance company's computer to type the requested information directly into the insurance company's on-line system, entirely bypassing any data capture facilities provided by the agency's automation system. Interactive interface is most appropriate for:

- Agency inquiry into the insurance company's database for such items as policy status, coverage information, billing and payment data, and claims data
- Agency access to special company programs, such as rating, that are not supported on the agency's automation system
- Providing agents with the ability to resolve issues associated with complex commercial risks with a company underwriter while both access the same screens from their terminals

Interactive interface began when insurance companies placed dumb terminals in agency offices in the 1970s. Exhibit 3-2 illustrates this type

Exhibit 3-2
Company Terminal Interface

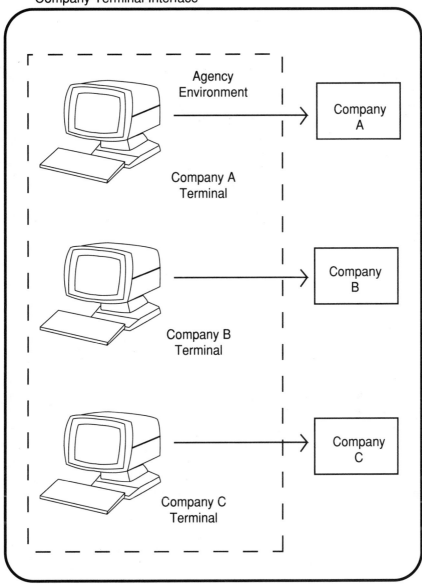

of interface, which is commonly referred to as the *company terminal* or *proprietary interface*—interface with one insurance company through facilities provided by that insurer. The agency can also use its own agency management system's terminals, rather than terminals provided by insurers, to access the insurance company's computer systems. Exhibit 3-3 illustrates a modified company terminal interface approach. In this configuration, the agency's terminals connect to its AMS and with insurers directly or through a network facility.

Advantages. There are a number of advantages to interactive interface. It requires little additional investment in software by the company to extend its home and field office systems to many agencies. With interactive interface, the company is free to make changes to existing products and to introduce new products without any dependence on one or more agency automation vendors to update their systems. Interactive interface gives the agency immediate access to selected portions of the insurance company's database to request policy and claim information, in turn permitting agencies to provide better customer service. The agency can enter data directly into the company's system where errors of omission and commission can be detected and flagged for immediate correction.

Disadvantages. Interactive interface has several disadvantages. The terms *multiple-entry interface* and *double-entry interface* are often used to refer to an interactive interface arrangement, since, in many cases, the data entered into the insurance company's computer is not automatically entered into the agency's in-house system. The information must be re-entered separately into the agency's in-house system. In addition to duplicate data entry, training, on an ongoing basis, is required to keep agency employees up to date as new system features are added or new employees are hired. Training complexity may also result in reliance or dependence on a small number of agency employees. The screens and procedures used to interface with insurers are not standardized for the most part. Some of the screens may not be very user-friendly or agency-oriented. Keys on the keyboard may have different definitions among the companies providing interactive interface to the agency. As a result, the agency must maintain operating manuals for each line of business and for each insurer with which it has interactive interface. These manuals are used to interpret company-specific terminology and codes often used in screen formats and messages.

Single-Entry Interface. *Single-entry* or *single-entry multiple company interface,* illustrated in Exhibit 3-4, allows entry of data once into the agency computer where it is stored until all of the activity for a given period, usually a day, is grouped (batched) together by company and transmitted (forwarded) to the agency's companies for processing. *Batch interface* and *batch store-and-forward interface* are other terms commonly used to describe single-entry interface. *Interactive up / batch back* is a type of single-entry interface in which data is entered interac-

Exhibit 3-3
Modified Company Terminal Interface

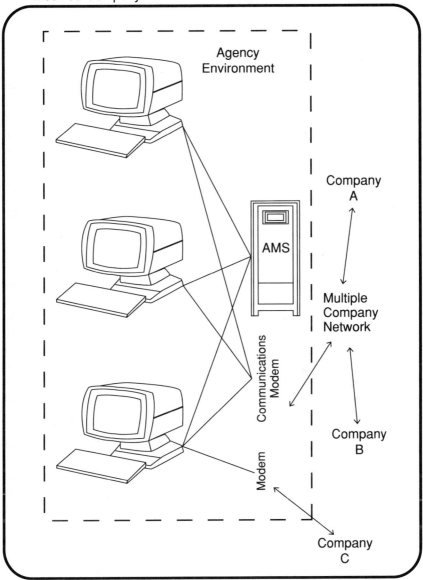

tively into the company system and is sent back to the agency's system in batch form with the batch transmission updating the agency's database. Single-entry interface that supports only one of the agency's companies is another example of a proprietary interface.

Exhibit 3-4

Single-Entry/Multiple Company Interface Through the AMS

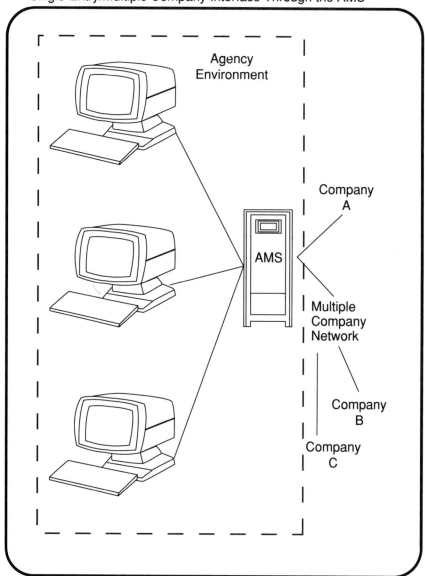

Advantages. Single-entry interface eliminates the costs, delays, and potential errors that can result when data is entered twice—once into the insurer's system and then again into the agency's system. Communication costs are lower than those of interactive interface, since data transmissions can take place at off-peak periods when telephone and network rates are lower. Screen formats are generated by the agency computer and are standardized for all companies and functions, reducing training time and improving agency productivity. Company-originated data updates the agency database without the need for data entry within the agency.

Disadvantages. There are several disadvantages associated with single-entry or batch-store-and-forward interface. The response to a transaction is not immediate. Even though a transaction is processed the evening after being entered into the agency computer, it may be several days before the policy documents confirming the successful processing of the transaction arrive in the mail. There is a delay in correcting errors. Agency data rejected by the company computer cannot be immediately corrected as it can under interactive interface. Software costs may be extensive for both the agency and/or company, especially if a company has to ask an agency automation software vendor to modify its system to accommodate company specific data not already captured by the vendor's system. From the company's stand-point, the task of adding interface with different vendors can represent a slow process of negotiation and software development, perhaps even slower if the automation vendor is owned by a competitor. The long-term costs of ongoing software maintenance are expected to be substantial.

Appropriate Uses. Single-entry or batch store-and-forward interface is most appropriate for high volume transactions in which the data are required by both the agency and company databases and in which the data requirements are straightforward and stable. Applications, endorsements, and cancellations are examples of this type of transaction. It is also appropriate for electronic mail applications in which agency and company personnel exchange messages, replacing FAX, telephones, mail, or express mail services.

Both interactive interface and single-entry interface are required for effective agency/company interface. Single-entry interface has the greatest potential for reducing the cost of delivering the insurance product by reducing the duplication of effort that currently exists. Before that potential can be realized, a great deal of additional work must still be completed.

Obstacles to Full Interface

Full-scale interface capability for personal and commercial lines of insurance among agencies and their companies is many years away.

Hardware and software operational standards must be developed and data entry, integrity, and expense issues must be resolved before full interface can be achieved successfully. The manner in which these issues are resolved will determine the competitive differences in interface capabilities among insurers. For interface to produce a more efficient insurance process, companies and agencies must determine anew what insurance functions are best handled in the agency and what functions are best handled by the companies.

Hardware and Software Operational Issues. Single-entry, multiple-company interface "requires the agency to use and manage a 'full function,' full database of all client coverage detail on the agency management system." [5] Not only must agencies acquire sufficiently powerful hardware and software, but companies must also expand their automation activities and attain or approach the status of the fully automated or "paperless" office. Even when the necessary systems are in place, daily operational problems still require ongoing management. System failures always have and always will occur in the agency system, the telecommunications network, or company system. The remedy requires the development of complex error handling, error recovery, and system restart procedures. Software changes made by insurance companies or agency automation vendors will have to be thoroughly tested and coordinated so that interface facilities do not fail or cause erroneous results.

Standards. Uniform standards must be established for the way the information is organized and for the form in which it is transmitted between company and agency computers. An organization known as ACORD, discussed below, provides such standards for the insurance industry. ACORD coordinates the time-consuming, complex, and expensive process of developing standards for the type of information being transmitted. Standards allow agency system vendors and companies to modify their systems or develop conversion programs to reformat standard information to the vendor system and company system requirements.

Another standards-related issue is the divergence in standard implementation procedures among owners of an agency automation system. Agency A may have the latest version of all ACORD standards, while Agency B has the current version for personal lines and a prior version for commercial lines. In effect, communication between company and agency must be preceded by an agency interface status report.

Data Entry and Integrity. The most cost-effective location for the data entry function is in the agency. There are two types of data entry arrangements: one using online interactive interface and the other using single-entry or batch store-and-forward processing. Errors will always occur during the entry of data. With online interactive interface, agency employees can correct errors as they occur during data entry. However, as noted earlier, interactive interface results in redundant processing. Data is entered in the agency twice, once when online with the insurer and then again to update the agency's own information system. Errors occur when the data is not entered identically in both entry operations.

The advantage of single-entry interface is offset by the limited ability to edit and check the agency data at the time it is being entered in the system. The result can be that single entry interface generates a substantial volume of communications back and forth between the company and agency to correct mistakes before the data can be processed by the company's systems.

Another aspect of the data entry issue is the synchronization of data among company and agency automation systems. Much of the information on clients, policies, and claims already exists or will exist in automation systems of both agency and insurer. It will be some time before standards defining the data to be returned to the agency from insurers (policy numbers, rates, premium, expiration dates, status information, and so on) are implemented by all interfacing companies and agencies. Until such time, the manual updating of information on an agency's system must be handled with care to ensure that incorrect information is not sent to a company when the agency creates an endorsement transaction.

Costs.   There are a number of costs associated with agency/company interface. These costs include communication hardware and software, memory and possible terminal enhancements to the agency system and the cost of the communication line from the agency's modem to the network or directly to the carrier. There will also be charges for actual network usage, as well as the storage of data within the network prior to its retrieval by a company or agency. Some services and products (rating software, modifications to agency automation software to capture company unique data, and telecommunication or network usage costs) may be considered a necessary business expense and be absorbed by the insurers. Other costs (automation and interface hardware and software benefiting the agency and all of the other insurance companies the agency represents) benefit the agency more than the insurers represented. Insurers may assist agencies in bearing such costs, perhaps on the basis of volume commitments.

At this writing, agency/company interface should still be considered unsettled. Even though most of the activity taking place is in the interactive interface mode and the return on insurer investment in interface is low, the number of interface functions is growing and the consensus of both agencies and companies is that single-entry, multiple company interface can be achieved. Insurance company marketing departments also continue to place tremendous emphasis on interface. Their reason is that they are both hopeful and fearful that their key agencies will limit the companies they represent to those with interface capabilities.

ACORD

Evolution

ACORD, an industry-wide organization, plays a key role in the evolution of interface in the property and liability insurance industry. The name ACORD is now attached to an organization that is the outgrowth of other organizations, one of which originally bore the name ACORD.

The Agency-Company Operations Research and Development Corporation, ACORD, was organized in 1970 as the result of activities of the Independent Insurance Agents and Brokers of California. Its purpose was to standardize the paper forms used for routine insurance procedures. It addressed a problem acknowledged throughout the industry: insurance companies all had their own application, claims, and other forms. This led to a variety of problems and inefficiencies, particularly within agencies that served a number of insurers. The numerous standard forms and procedure guides developed by ACORD are in widespread use throughout the insurance industry. They provided the groundwork of paper standards on which electronic standards were later built.

In 1978 the industry created the Insurance Institute for Research (IIR) to address the issue of electronic standardization. The founding participants were the Independent Insurance Agents of America's Electronic Process Implementation Committee (EPIC) and twenty major property and liability insurance companies. The scope of IIR research was broad. It included rating systems on personal computers, semi-automated procedures in agencies, fully automated agencies, and automation in insurance companies. IIR brought into being an electronic network facility, IVANS, to be described shortly. IVANS is now a separate organization.

Industry leaders recognized the interdependence of paper and electronic standards. IIR and ACORD merged in 1983, forming a new nonprofit corporation, IIR/ACORD. In 1987 IIR/ACORD changed its name to ACORD. This simplification symbolized the full unification of the original IIR and ACORD organizations and the concentration of paper and electronic standards development in a single center.

Mission

The ACORD effort to establish data processing standards is of sweeping significance to the insurance industry. Using existing ACORD paper documents as a starting point, electronic transaction formats are defined. That is, there are standardized requirements for the sequence of each piece of data and the way each is expressed, e.g., insured vehicle. Through the development of standards, ACORD attempts to establish a common framework for interface software development. Two types of standards are involved. Batch store-and-forward standards define data record formats or layouts, not as they would be stored internally in agency and company computers, but as they would be transmitted between them. Interactive standards, on the other hand, involve data that can be seen by the agency system's users. Interactive standards define screen formats and the human/machine interactions to be displayed on the screens of company terminals located in the agency.

Despite the unquestioned gains that result from ACORD effort, interface will not completely standardize the industry. There will always be different ways of doing the same thing. With standards implemented, 70 to 80 percent of company information will be captured, but the other 20 to 30 percent will be specialized insurer underwriting and rating data. The unique information will be handled individually for each agency automation vendor or through the reduction of extraneous underwriting data requirements by the insurers.

ACORD has been very successful in meeting its objectives. Its agency automation guide and hotline service are designed to help agents apply computer technology as well as assess its value to their business. ACORD published standards for the transmission protocol, or electronic envelope, which contains identifying information for both the sender and recipient of the transmission. Published standards for the contents of the electronic envelope include personal and commercial lines transactions, electronic memos, and the definition of print images. More standards are under development. In addition to its role in promulgating standards, ACORD has evolved an educational role. Through seminars and publications, ACORD fosters an understanding of interface and, more broadly, insurance automation.

IVANS

Evolution

In 1981, the Insurance Institute for Research created an ad hoc committee to explore the feasibility of an industrywide telecommunications network. Working with a consultant, the committee developed a proposal which was distributed to a number of vendors offering networking solutions. The IBM Information Network, IBM/IN, was initially chosen to provide the telecommunications services. The committee also recommended that an organization or company, separate from ACORD, be formed to manage the industrywide network. In January, 1983, IVANS came into existence to furnish a property and liability industry telecommunications facility.

IVANS is a nonprofit corporation, owned and operated by its members. It is charged with the responsibility of satisfying the data transmission needs of its member companies and the agents with whom they do business. As the management entity, IVANS assures that the services provided by IBM/IN and other firms meet its members' requirements. By representing its members as a single entity, IVANS is able to make its members beneficiaries of substantial volume discounts. In addition, by acting collectively, IVANS members are able to exercise significant economic persuasion on network providers to offer services they need.

Value Added Services

In addition to providing telecommunication capabilities, IVANS also offers other *value added services*. In order to understand the meaning of value added services, it is necessary to understand what a data network provides.

A data network functions very much like a (voice) telephone network. It provides the medium for an agency computer equipped with the proper communication hardware and software to interface with other interconnected computers at multiple locations. Usage charges are normally based on the *connect time* that a computer is tied or linked into a network, the number of characters transmitted, and the value added functions utilized. Traditionally, value added carriers such as IVANS and IBM Information Network lease underlying transmission facilities from AT&T and other common carriers.

IVANS adds value to basic telephone services by offering speed, protocol (communication standards) conversions, and other functions to provide users with enhanced data communication services. In other words, IVANS permits otherwise incompatible terminals and computers to communicate with one another and ensures the integrity of data transmission by means of sophisticated error detection and correction techniques.

The key value added feature of IVANS is batch store-and-forward communications. Batch store-and-forward reduces the communication capacity required of an agency or company. Neither is required to support the telecommunications hardware to handle communication at peak periods. Communications are simplified. The agency or company does not have to dial and redial the other's computer because of a busy signal. The sender of the communication simply connects with IVANS and transmits its messages. The messages are held in the recipient's in-basket until the receiver connects with IVANS to collect it.

The format conversion facility is another key feature offered by IVANS. This feature provides insurers with the ability to translate the data contained in the batch store-and-forward transactions received from an agency into the form and sequence their computers expect it to be in. Where an insurer does not have an automated system, in some commercial lines for example, the format conversion facility can create a paper application which can be processed by the underwriter just as if it had been received through the mail. Insurers also use the format conversion facility to translate the data they send to their interfaced agencies into a form that can be accepted by the agency computers, since not all agency systems will support every standard in the same way or at the same time.

The interactive communication feature allows agencies and companies to use IVANS in a pass-through mode for communications as a substitute for dedicated leased lines normally used for company terminals. The network may perform some protocol and speed conversions in the process, but essentially it allows an agency to access a company's online system using the agency's computer terminal or personal computer.

Outlook for the Future

The number of interfacing agents and companies continues to grow. At this writing, many interfacing arrangements are proprietary interactive interfaces between an agency and a company. Single-entry interface is still relatively infrequent and concentrated on personal lines homeowners and automobile new business transactions.

A great deal of work remains to be completed by agencies, agency automation vendors, insurance companies, ACORD, and IVANS. However, the process is well under way and has good momentum. It is expected that there will be a steady expansion of interactive-up/batch-back interface, utilizing a mix of interactive and batch store-and-forward transmissions. Some transactions will always require immediate answers interactively; but most will probably be handled through a single-entry, batch store-and-forward process to achieve the expected saving. In sum, there will be a variety of interface arrangements in use in the insurance industry.

COMPUTERS, THE INSURANCE INDUSTRY, AND THE FUTURE

The chapter has thus far looked at past and current uses of computers in the insurance industry. We will now speculate on the insurance industry's use of computers in the future.

Potential for the Insurance Industry

The potential for computerization in the insurance industry is enormous and indeed challenging. There are several concepts or goals that seem to capture the attention of those who observe the insurance data processing scene.

Paperless Processing.   Many vendors marketing to the insurance industry stress achievements toward the goal of paperless processing. The amount of insurance resources—money and labor—that goes toward managing paper makes clear why this is a worthwhile goal.

Advocates of paperless processing point to the concept that a piece of paper is merely one medium for storing information. Information in the insurance company has always been stored on paper—policy terms, changes to contracts, applications, and other related items. This is because paper has been, historically, the favored medium for maintaining permanent records. Since computers can now store information more economically than it can be stored on paper, why not store all information in the computer?

Some companies are moving quickly in this direction. Software vendors have made great strides in reducing reliance on paper documents, but we are still a long way from paperless processing. The trend from transaction-oriented systems to policy-oriented systems was the first step toward this goal. Many companies achieved some relief from the paper avalanche by adopting microfilm data storage. Others have shied away from it on grounds that it detracts from efforts toward automation through computers.

Image processing, under development for some time and now in use in a few companies, offers hope to those who seek a paperless insurance industry. Image processing involves the translation of the image of a piece of paper into a series of digits which can be stored in digital form. It will probably be a few years before image processing is generally affordable. Storage requirements are immense and will probably be met by laser disk technology, much like that now used in audio compact disk players. A laser disk twelve inches in diameter can hold up to two billion characters, or the equivalent of more than a million double-spaced typewritten pages.

The effect of image processing on insurance company operations will be great. Underwriters will be able to see photographs of homes and businesses on the screens of their terminals and personal computers. Claims employees will be able to view police reports, notices of loss, and photographs of the accident scenes and the vehicles involved on their screens rather than shuffling through their files. With split-screen displays, underwriters may have an image of the policy application in one window and a photograph of the home in another window, while working with the company's policy processing system in a third. Image processing technology will allow policyholder information to be accessed by several people at the same time; in addition, it will speed access to documents, and reduce the floor space and labor costs associated with manual paper filing systems.

User-Directed System. Perhaps no other single development has been as interesting as the emerging role of end users. Insurance systems are no longer designed and implemented by just the technically oriented information system specialists. Projects today are much too large and complex for that. Instead, users and data processors alike are working together on project teams to bring major system efforts to fruition.

Future systems are most likely to be user-directed to a great extent. This will be brought about, first of all, by widespread use of user-oriented programming languages. As these languages become more and more like the English language, a greater number of users will take advantage of them. This will lead to a greater independence from the information system department of the company. Users, conscious of growing pains and problems in past computer development, seem eager to deepen their involvement. As the fourth-generation languages increase in their power, the trend toward user direction will be intensified.

Another factor adding to greater computer direction by users is the emphasis on distributed data processing. While user-oriented languages give the user the power to operate the computer, distributed data processing puts the computer where users can take advantage of that power.

This picture is paradoxical, however. As systems are becoming more oriented to the user, they will, at the same time, become more complex; and as user languages become more powerful, more functions will be added to the operating software, making the operating software more complex. That portion of the computer that must be used to keep the systems software operating (as opposed to the applications programs) is referred to as *overhead*. This overhead also increases as distributed data processing is implemented.

While some of this overhead may be transferred away from the main computer location, the overall computer system has become more difficult to manage. Thus, users will be directing more of the system than ever before, but they will be limited to those options by the operating system software. Ultimately, control, as opposed to immediate usage of systems, will probably reside with fewer people rather than with more.

The Electronic Office. When does a typewriter stop being a typewriter and become a computer? The answer to this question lies in the additional functions that may be performed by the typewriter, such as information storage or text editing. As computers have grown smaller, typewriters have grown larger—at least in the number of functions they provide. With the introduction of the IBM Magnetic Tape/Selectric Typewriter in 1964, the word processing industry was off to a flying start. Since then innovations have come along rapidly. Some "typewriters" available today are actually small special-purpose minicomputers complete with video display. By the end of the century, voice-activated typewriters and PCs may appear in company and agency offices. These machines will turn speech into text.

Rising labor costs for clerks, typists, and similar workers have led to an increased demand for office machines, and rapidly developing computer circuit technology has led to an enticing array of devices. The whole idea of an electronic office is similar to, and related to, the concepts of agency-company terminal networks and paperless processing. Widespread use of optical recognition equipment allows documents to be read immediately into the computer system, in either the agency or the underwriter's office. Computer output will be printed directly on microfilm for convenient long-term storage. Facsimile transmission allows documents to be transferred over telephone lines. Faster transfer times and, therefore, lower long distance telephone costs should lead to realization of the electronic mail concept. Voice communications through computers are seen as a future reality. Voice synthesis, the process of turning automated text into speech, is expected to be commercialized by the end of the century.

The future of the office in American business tends to arouse the imagination. Some fear the loss of the "personal touch" while others fear that automation will not come fast enough. Experience with computers and related equipment to date, however, suggests that technology will probably develop faster than our ability to manage it. The capabilities of computers are likely to exceed the ability to manage and effectively use those capabilities. The office of the future, therefore, waits not on the delivery of the machinery, but rather on the arrival of managers capable of its management.

MIS for the Insurance Company

Early attempts toward management information system (MIS) development in the insurance industry generally resembled MIS development as a whole. There was, as expected, disenchantment with the MIS concept for some time among insurance company managers. This is changing as information database systems are being operated successfully by many companies. The success of software vendors, with their policy-oriented package programs, has also shown skeptics that there may yet be hope for the MIS concept, at least in some modified form.

Although online, policy-oriented systems seem to have been designed around processing needs, rather than management information needs, they do offer a base of data that can be fed to a controlling management information system. At the least, these systems offer the groundwork for the design of a management information system.

For many companies, the purchased database system is the chosen approach to MIS. This represents a "bottom-up" approach to MIS development. After mastering routine data processing functions, the system can move "upward" toward more sophisticated utilization of management information. Although attending to processing needs first, the purchased database system collects much information that is management information as part of the process. After the bulk of processing data has been collected, the information services staff can work toward obtaining management information that is not already part of the database.

Other companies have utilized the growing expertise of software vendors in developing a management information system. The underlying idea here is that the vendors will continue to increase the functions and overall capabilities of their systems. Moreover, the information retained in their MIS, as with the more general database systems, will continue to grow in quantity and scope. With the vendor responsible for improving and maintaining its software, the company programming staff is free to concentrate on those computer information needs that are unique to the organization. In most cases, the unique needs will be management information needs.

The currently popular way to MIS involves a federation of systems rather than a grand design. Regardless of the method used by the company (purchased database system, purchased applications software system, or company-developed systems), the incremental approach seems to be the practice among insurers today.

Roadblocks to Progress

The pathway to increasing automation of the insurance industry has both the initial allure and the ultimate perils of the yellow brick road. Before one can get to the Land of Oz, many hurdles must be overcome. Moreover, in the end, the wizardry promised by the computer may be found to have been an illusion fed by our insistent wish for it to be real. There are some roadblocks which must be analyzed to determine if they warrant major or minor shifts in the journey toward computerization. A few of them will be introduced here. The key word in the previous sentence is "introduced." The intent is to make the reader aware of the issues. Solutions will require much discussion and debate.

The Problem of Information Ineffectiveness. [6] Despite all of the attention directed towards information management and the technical advances in information delivery, many insurance executives often find themselves without all of the information they need to manage their businesses. As a result of the incremental approach to developing a comprehensive management information system, many insurance companies periodically find themselves in the position of being "data rich" and "information poor." Their systems capture the right data but may not deliver the information executives need to achieve effectiveness in their management functions. In addition, needed information might be too late, it might be organized the wrong way, and it might conflict with information contained in special, one-time reports.

There are several hurdles insurance company executives and information systems staffs must overcome if executives and managers are to monitor and manage the company's progress toward its strategic goals:

- *Lack of understanding and agreement on objectives and priority tasks.* This hurdle can be resolved by identifying the key areas of activity in which favorable results are absolutely necessary for the company to reach its goals and address its key priorities.

Doing so can help the whole organization understand and focus on the company's strategic direction.

- *Information not linked to management processes.* Management and operating procedures must not only be linked to the right information, but they may also have to be redesigned, if necessary, to support and motivate the appropriate management behavior.
- *Shifting thoughts on information needs.* Clarifying executive information requirements is a trial-and-error process that fosters an executive's learning, thinking, and intuitive understanding of problems. The ideal information system is flexible and responsive to the needs of its users and yet seems orderly and comprehensible to them.

Overcoming these barriers will be a repetitive process. The information problem raises its head each time markets and insurance cycles are influenced by shifting competitive forces and executives are forced to evaluate their company's strategic direction.

Security Concerns. [7] The subject of computer security has received much attention in the press. The concern for security of the computer and the information stored in the computer system is very much on the minds of corporate executives. As investments in computer systems increase, concern should intensify.

Loss or damage to computers and their data can occur in several ways. Computers are subject to fire, lightning, and other familiar perils. Moreover, especially with the larger computers, sudden changes in temperature or humidity can result in loss. Vandalism is also a significant peril. Some destruction is done solely out of malice while some extremist groups, knowing the high potential for loss in data centers, destroy them to gain recognition. Many companies have installed expensive protective equipment to guard against these threats. No longer is the computer likely to be on display in a glass walled room. It may be placed in the most remote location possible. Computer crime also produces losses. Crimes, in some cases, are committed for the challenge of "beating the computer system" rather than for any monetary gain. Nevertheless, extremely large sums have been embezzled with the aid of computers.

The issue for the insurance industry, as well as for other industries, is the trade-off between the savings of computerization and the chance of damage or loss of significant company information. Few people are willing to say that computerization should be halted to reduce the company's vulnerability to a major loss. Some point to the enormous risk created when there is a centralized database with all corporate information. Despite elaborate security measures, there is still no absolute protection of the corporate database. What is an acceptable level of risk of theft, destruction, or misuse of the database? How can this risk be weighed against the competitive necessity and savings involved? Distributing the database (as under distributed data processing) reduces the problem but does not eliminate it. Because of our growing dependence on computers, future computer system designs will reflect a growing concern for computer and data security.

Privacy Concerns.[8] The issue of computer privacy has become a major public concern. It is commonly accepted that organizations require more information from us now than ever before. Government requirements for paper work from businesses have grown at a staggering rate. Insurance statistical organizations capture and maintain massive amounts of information. With the growing use of computer networks, many people are concerned about the misuse of information stored in computers.

Privacy legislation has been passed in the United States and in several western European countries. The concern for privacy is not new. What is new is the ability of government and sometimes other organizations to obtain and control large amounts of data about individuals through the use of computers. Personnel data stored in the computer might conceivably be accessed by an unauthorized party using a terminal.

Opinions on computer privacy tend to fall into one of three categories. First, there are those very concerned about the invasion of privacy possible with computers. Second, there are those who feel that the first group is making much ado about nothing and are more concerned about the cost and restraints that may be placed on computer departments due to privacy legislation. Third, many people are simply not aware of the issue.

Maintenance of privacy in computer systems costs money. Some argue that the privacy question should be decided on the basis of a cost/benefit analysis. The problem with this approach is putting a dollar figure on the benefits of maintaining the privacy of citizens. Insurance companies are sensitive to the matter since they maintain a great deal of personal information about policyholders.

When examining agency-company interface, one must consider the rights of each policyholder to the privacy of personal information. Similarly, companies must not be able to extract private agency information from the network. And company pricing or financial data must not flow through the network to agencies or to other insurers.

In a normal situation, privacy would probably not be difficult to safeguard, for each insurer has a competitive interest in protecting its data. But what about an abnormal situation? It is difficult for many of us in this country to envision how an unscrupulous person or group might use large computer databases to influence or control portions of the population. It is not the probability of personal data being misused that causes worry, but the mere possibility of major misuse of personal data stored in computers.

Those who develop insurance systems will have to consider this issue because of the legislation it has produced—if for no other reason. The insurance industry will benefit, though, if thoughtful leaders step forward to provide guidance on this complex issue. The privacy issue provides the insurance industry with an opportunity to assert leadership in the business world in a matter of national importance.

Cost Allocation. Automation continues to change the process of providing insurance. The traditional allocation of functions between agency and company are eroded as the computer enables—even compels—reassignment of some functions. For instance, the agency is likely to perform more of the underwriting functions as the agency computer, interfaced with the insurer's computer, has access to information used in simple underwriting decisions. How much should the agency be paid for performing these functions? Obviously, agencies will seek larger commissions when processing and storage functions are shifted from company to agency. Companies will seek to reduce commission rates as they perform decision, processing, and storage functions previously performed in the agency.

Cost allocation is a major issue in another way, too. The achievement of a full industry-wide agency/company interface will carry an enormous price tag. What is a fair split between companies and agencies? Should development costs be allocated to all firms in the insurance industry? Or should some firms be allowed a free (or, at least, cheap) ride as they follow in the footsteps of the brave?

TYPICAL DAY IN THE FUTURE

In tomorrow's automated agency, agency staff members will process their work through their own automated systems, moving in and out of multiple *windows* of information on the screens. The windows will allow the agency staff to see and relate information from client, policy, loss, diary, note pad, word processing, and interface files on the screen all at once. The windows will be moved around on the screen, just as the agency staff now moves paper, and will be made larger, made smaller, or will disappear depending on the current task or inquiry from a client. As they are processed, those transactions which require action by an insurer will be identified for subsequent transmission to one or more companies and placed in the agency's interface out-basket. At a convenient time during the day the accumulated transactions will be transmitted through local telephone lines to the closest IVANS access point for distribution to the companies to whom the transactions are addressed. From time to time, agency staff will activate various windows on their workstation screens to obtain comparative rates based on information already contained in the system's client and policy files, to write letters and memos to insureds and prospects, or to project the results of today's events on the agency's financial position at some time in the future.

Periodically throughout the day, or at the end of each day, the companies will collect the accumulated transactions from IVANS and bring them in to their own internal automation systems. Prescreening or computer-assisted underwriting systems developed using expert systems technology will separate those transactions requiring manual review from the ones that can be processed without additional human intervention. The prescreening process will also generate requests for motor vehicle reports, credit and inspection reports, Insurance Services Office (ISO) survey data, and basic fire rates. Once the prescreening process is completed, the flow of transactions through the processing cycle of the company will be controlled by *queues*. The processing workload, identified by activity as it enters the company's automation system, will be queued for processing by underwriting, rating, claims or document processing. By searching the work queues, any underwriter will be able to determine his or her current workload. The underwriter can then schedule the work and proceed to process it.

The screens at underwriter workstations will also be divided into windows. The underwriter will move in and out of multiple windows to relate credit reports, inspection reports, agency comments and risk analysis, rating, diary, and scratch pad notes to the application being evaluated. When presented with a complex commercial account, local underwriters will schedule telephone conferences to review the risk with more experienced underwriters through their respective screens, no matter where they are located geographically. When underwriting has completed its evaluation of the transaction, the information will be placed in a rating queue. Rating will process its work according to effective change date. Using computerized rating systems, premium calculations and statistical codes will be developed after which the policy will be released for printing either within the company's location or directed for transmission to the agency for printing. Claim processing will be handled in a similar manner. Once the information request or transaction has been processed by the company, status information and any documents to be printed in the agency office will be electronically communicated to IVANS or other networks for storage until collected by the agency system. The agency system will then update the client policy and loss files as needed. The agency staff members will then be able to review the information through a window, or print out the information, memos, policy documents, and forms on the agency's printer for distribution within the agency and mailing to the client.

As we see, the typical insurance office day in the future looks neither futuristic nor frightening. Computers and networks, including those that provide interface between agencies and companies, will handle almost all messages. They will be the same messages that now flow along slower channels. This scenario shows a little room for the relocation of functions, but does not suggest any drastic shift of tasks from company to agency or vice versa. It promises major benefits: greater efficiency, economy, speed, and accuracy. One step at a time, the insurance industry will bring this scenario to life.

SUMMARY

The history of the computer in the insurance industry has not been unique, but there are some ways in which the industry has made its special mark on the use of computers. Insurance companies were among the first to jump on the computer bandwagon. Having the necessary funds and the potential for major expense reduction, insurers stepped quickly to purchase the bulky and expensive computers of the late 1950s and early 1960s. Many sensed that the computer could fill some very big needs within the insurance company, but few people realized that the computer field would develop as fast as it has.

Insurance companies are now among the major users of computer power. Sophistication has increased dramatically. From the early monofunctional systems to today's multi-purpose integrated systems the leaps have been nothing short of staggering. In the insurance company of today, the information services department plays a role of enormous significance.

The insurance agency, aided by the growth of service bureaus and by the emergence of the minicomputer, joined the computerization race in the 1970s. With outside vendors providing most of the expertise for the typical smaller agency, computerization first spread at a modest pace. Computerization of agencies accelerated when insurers established agency automation assistance programs and took ownership positions in vendor companies. Perhaps the most discussed topic in insurance data processing circles today is the agency/company interface picture.

The potential for use of the computer in the insurance industry seems almost limitless because of the nature of the internal operations of insurers, and the large amounts of data flowing from one department to another. The computer offers the promise of reducing the problems associated with the high volume of paper work. Many look forward to paperless processing, realization of a fully effective MIS, the electronic office, and other concepts.

Yet without doubt some obstacles stand in the way of complete and effective computerization. One is the inability to improve management and decision-making capacity at the same pace as improvements in computer technology. There is need to integrate the standalone systems that abound within insurance organizations. Agency/company interface is marked by diversity and disappointment. True, there exists the nationwide agency/company data communications network the industry first asked for in 1978. The challenge for insurers and agency automation vendors is to develop the capability to use the network to improve the industry's efficiency.

The security, privacy, and cost allocation concerns which the computer causes must be dealt with while providing insurance policies and service in a competitive arena. It is almost certain that the insurance industry can survive as a private industry only if it can cut the costs of delivering its products. There seems to be no alternative to more effective computer utilization that will permit this reduction. All things considered, the insurance industry's future with the computer should be even more lively and interesting than its past.

Chapter Notes

1. Bernard L. Webb, J.J. Launie, Willis Park Rokes, and Norman A. Baglini, *Insurance Company Operations*, Vol. I. (Malvern, PA: American Institute for Property and Liability Underwriters, 1978), p. 81.
2. Robert J. Anderson, Eileen B. Hamburg, William F. McGahan, and Alan J. Turner, *Automation in Insurance* (Malvern, PA: Insurance Institute of America, 1988), pp. 62-66.
3. Richard G. Canning, ed., "Making Office Systems Pay Off," *EDP Analyzer* (February 1985), pp. 8-12.
4. Insurance Institute for Research, *Agency Automation Guide,* 1978.
5. John McCauley, "A Look at Interface," *Independent Agent,* September 1988, p. 77.
6. Holly Gunner and Gary K. Gulden, "Partnerships Between Executives and Information Professionals Speed Business Strategy Execution," *Information Management Review,* Spring 1986, pp. 12-18.
7. F. Warren McFarlan and Richard L. Nolan, eds., *The Information Systems Handbook* (Homewood, IL: Dow Jones-Irwin, Inc., 1975), pp. 832-842.
8. McFarlan and Nolan, pp. 843-856.

Glossary

ACORD—An organization that provides technical standards for electronic interface among insurance organizations.

Acoustic Coupler—A device that allows a telephone to be used to provide communication from a terminal to a computer via a telephone network. An acoustic coupler is a type of modem that transfers information to a telephone line using sound impulses rather than direct electrical connection.

Add-on Memory—An additional primary storage unit attached to the CPU to, in effect, enlarge the size of primary storage.

ADP—See Automatic Data Processing

ALU—See Arithmetic/Logic Unit

Analog Computer—A computer that measures continuously variable data. Compare Digital Computer.

Applications Programming—Programming concerned with business problems as opposed to internal requirements of the computer. Compare Systems Programming.

Applications Software—Those programs that address business problems, such as accounts receivable, forecasting and word processing, as opposed to internal requirements of the computer. Compare Systems Software.

Arithmetic/Logic Unit—That unit within the CPU in which arithmetic and logical comparison functions take place.

Artificial Intelligence—The ability of a computer to perform tasks characteristic of human intelligence, such as learning from experience and reasoning.

ASCII (American Standard Code for Information Exchange)—The code used to represent letters, numbers, and other characters in data transmission.

Assembler—The software that translates a symbolic language program into a machine language program that the computer can process.

Assembler Language—A symbolic programming language. Each computer usually has its own assembler language.

Assembly Program—A computer program written in assembly language.

Asynchronous—A type of data transmission that uses start and stop elements for each character. Compare bisynchronous and synchronous.

Automatic Data Processing—The field of computers and related work.

Auxiliary Memory—Storage media (for instance, disk or tape) other than primary storage.

Auxiliary Storage—Same as Auxiliary Memory.

Back-Up—(1) A copy of a computer file (tape, disk) that is retained in order to provide a means of recovery from system failure. (2) Back-up facility: another computer on which programs can be run in the event of extended sytem hardware failure.

BASIC (Beginner's All-purpose Symbolic Instruction Code)—A procedure oriented programming language that is widely used in timesharing operations.

Batch—An accumulation of data that is considered a unit (as a day's sales) to be processed at one time in a computer system or communications network. Interactive processing is an alternative.

Batch Processing—Processing in which data is grouped and submitted to the computer in batches. Compare Real-Time Processing.

Baud—For practical purposes, a term used in telecommunications as a unit of measure of data information flow. It stands for 1 *bit* per second. Divide by 8 to calculate characters per second.

Bisynchronous Transmission—A type of synchronous transmission developed by IBM (IBM Bisync).

Bit—Short for binary digit, that is, the smallest element of data in a computer.

Branch—The computer's ability to transfer from one part of a program (that is, to branch) to another part of the program based on the result of some comparison performed by the program.

Buffer—A part of a computer's memory where data can be stored until the computer is ready to process it. Some peripherals also have buffers.

Bugs—Any problems found in a software program which cause it to perform incorrectly.

Byte—A computer term for a character of information (D, 8, $, etc.). Computers are often compared in terms of memories expressed in thousands (K) or millions (megabytes—MB) of bytes. For example, a personal computer memory of 640K means that the computer's memory can hold approximately 640,000 characters.

Card Punch—A computer output device that produces the computer-readable medium of punched cards.

Card Reader—A computer input device that reads punched cards.

Cassette Tape—A data medium on some computers.

Cathode-Ray Tube (CRT)—A television-like screen on which data can be displayed; a computer terminal with such a screen. Also called Video Display Terminal (VDT).

Centralized Data Processing—Processing in which one host computer controls and services a network of terminals.

Central Processing Unit (CPU)—The heart of a computer system consisting of primary storage, arithmetic/logic, and control units.

Channels—Computer devices supporting the operation of the computer system.

Chip—An integrated circuit or integration of many circuits on a wafer slice, most often silicon, which contains these circuits.

COBOL (COmmon Business-Oriented Language)—Perhaps the most common procedure-oriented language in use today.

Code—When a computer program is written, it is often said to be coded. The written program instructions are called the code.

COM (Computer Output to Microfilm)—A technology combining electronic, photo-optical and electromechanical techniques for the purpose of converting digitized computer output into human-readable images and automatically recording these images on microfilm or microfiche.

Compiler—The software that translates a procedure-oriented language into machine language that the computer can execute.

Computer—A data processor that can perform computation, including numerous arithmetic or logic operations, without intervention by a human operator during the run.

Computer Science—The study of computers, with particular emphasis on their internal design and technological state.

Configuration—The design or layout of a particular computer system with all its peripherals. To configure a system is to design a system to meet specific needs. Can also mean to set certain hardware or software options in a manner which makes them compatible with the host.

Control Unit—That part of the central processing unit that exercises control over the functions performed by the computer.

Conversational—Same as Interactive.

Core—Another term for the primary storage of the central processing unit. The term reflects the fact that early storage units had a magnetic core as the prime component.

CP/M (Control Program for Microcomputers)—A disk operating system used by many manufacturers, and a trademark of Digital Research Corporation.

CPS (Characters Per Second)—A measurement of speed of character transmission or printing.

CPU—See Central Processing Unit.

CRT—See Cathode-Ray Tube.

Cursor—A position indicator on a CRT, usually a flashing rectangle or underscore.

Daisy Wheel Printer—A printing device characterized by high quality printing produced by direct impact of each character of type.

Data—Raw facts in isolation which, when placed in a meaningful context by a data processing operation(s), allow inference to be drawn. Compare Information.

Database—An organized collection of related files that contain data for the operation of an organization.

Data Center—The physical area and department or group of people associated with physical maintenance, operations and security of the computer itself. Sometimes called Operations.

Data Communications—Operations which transfer data from one terminal or processor to another terminal or processor, usually through telephone, microwave, or satellite technology.

Data Entry—The process of entering information into a computer system; for example, keying data into a terminal.

Data Processing (DP)—The field of computers and their related activity. Any procedure for receiving information and rearranging it to produce a specific result.

Data Processor—Any machine that performs operations with data.

DDP—See Distributed Data Processing.

Debugging—The process of correcting a computer program, including detection of errors and subsequent resolution of problems.

Decision Table—A documentation aid similar in purpose to a flowchart depicting in Matrix form (first) conditions that may occur in the program and (second) actions for the program to take based on the respective condition.

Dedicated Line—A telephone line used to transfer data in data communications that is leased and used solely for the purpose of transferring data between two points. A dedicated line eliminates the need for dialing, and the connection is thus permanent until disconnected. Compare Dial-Up Line.

Development Programming—Creating programs for the first time. Compare Maintenance Programming.

Dial-Up-Line—A telephone line used to transfer data from one point to another. The connection is made by dialing the number of the computer or other processor to receive the data. Each time data is to be transferred, dialing (making a connection) is required. Compare Dedicated Line.

Digital Computer—Computer that performs computations on noncontinuous, discrete data (that is, it uses digits). Compare Analog Computer.

Direct Access—The ability to retrieve data elements without reading the entire data file sequentially. Compare Sequential Access.

Direct-connect—Usually used with reference to modems, direct-connect describes a physical connection between the modem and modular telephone plug (as opposed to an acoustic connection, wherein a microphone and speaker connect to a telephone handset).

Disk—A metal or mylar disk with magnetic coating used to record information magnetically. Disk storage is the amount of information it can hold and is measured in millions (megabyte, MB) of characters.

Disk Drive—The device that contains and operates the disks.

Diskette (floppy disk)—A flexible mylar disk which is housed in a paper-like jacket. The data is stored magnetically but the total capacity is much lower than that of a hard disk. Microcomputers generally use 5¼" diskettes which are single or double sided with single or double density storage capabilities.

Disk Operating System (DOS)—A program used by the computer to read, write, and catalog disk files. Examples include MS/DOS and CP/M.

Disk Pack—A removable, direct access storage device containing magnetic disks on which data are stored.

Distributed Data Processing (DDP)—The permanent record describing the logic and other pertinent facts relating to a program or system. It may consist of flowcharts, decision tables, or other written documents.

Documentation—The permanent record describing the logic and other pertinent facts relating to a program or system. It may consist of flowcharts, decision tables, or other written documents.

DOS—See Disk Operating System.

Dot Matrix Printer (Wire Printer)—A high speed printer that prints character-like configurations of dots through the selection of wire-ends rather than conventional characters through the selection of type faces.

Downtime—That time which is lost when computer equipment is not working because of some malfunction.

DP—See Data Processing.

Dumb Terminal—A computer terminal with no processing capabilities of its own. Compare Intelligent Terminal.

Edit—A check performed by the computer or computer program for errors in data entered.

EDP—See Electronic Data Processing.

EFT—See Electronic Funds Transfer.

Electronic Cottage—See Telecommuting.

Electronic Data Processing (EDP)—The field of electronic computers and their operation.

Electronic Funds Transfer (EFT)—A banking procedure wherein money is transferred through a computer network utilizing data communications.

Electronic Mail—Mail sent in electronic form, not on paper.

End User—Persons who use computer outputs in an organization excluding members of the data processing department.

Ergonomics—The study of anatomical, physiological, and psychological aspects of people in their working environments.

Expert Systems—Computer programs that act as expert consultants to users. Expert systems consist of three components: a base of knowledge supplied by an expert in the field, a set of facts supplied by the user, and an inference capability supplied by the program.

Facilities Management—The subcontracting of an organization's entire data processing to another firm.

Floppy Disk—See Diskette.

FORTRAN (FORmula TRANslation)—A popular scientific-mathematic programming language.

Fourth Generation Languages—Languages that do not require the programmer to specify how to do everything to obtain the desired information from a computer. The programmer specifies what is to be done rather than how it is to be done.

Front-End Controller—Computer program used to feed work to the central processing unit by performing basic polling of all terminals in the network, relieving the CPU for other work.

General Purpose Computer—A computer able to perform a variety of functions. Compare Special Purpose Computer.

Generations—Term used to describe stages in the development of computers and their technology. Most analysts agree that there have been four or five generations of computers since they were introduced in the 1950s.

GO TO—Computer instruction that enables branching. The computer, when certain conditions occur, is able to *Go To* or *Branch To* some other part of the program.

Hard Copy—A computer printout on paper.

Hardware—Physical computer equipment. Compare Software.

High-Level Language—Same as Procedure-Oriented Language.

Host Computer—The controlling computer in a network of computer(s) and terminals.

Hybrid Computer—Computer with the characteristics of analog and digital computers.

Hybrid Processing—Processing which combines features of batch and online processing.

Icon—Symbol that represents procedures or devices desired.

Information—The increase in knowledge obtained by the recipient by matching the proper data elements to the variables of a problem. Information is the aggregation or processing of data to provide knowledge or intelligence. Compare Data.

Information Center—A department that offers aid to organization members in using their own information processing resources.

Information Processing—The field of computers and their management, particularly as related to business information systems.

Information Services (IS)—Department that provides information processing and coordinates development and use of information systems in an organization.

Ink-jet Printer—Non-impact printer that produces dot-matrix characters by spraying droplets of ink to form images.

Input—Data being entered into a system by a data entry device such as a CRT or by copying from a magnetic storage device such as a disk or tape. The process of entering data.

Intelligent Terminal—Computers used as terminals and thus having the capability to perform some processing functions. Compare Dumb Terminal.

Interactive Processing—Processing performed from a terminal with frequent person-machine interaction. As the computer receives input, it presents questions or instructions to the user, such as instructions for the next item of data to be entered.

Interface (general sense)—The electronic exchange of information.

Interface (in the insurance industry)—Electronic exchange of information between an agency computer system or terminal and the computer of an insurance company.

Internally Stored Program—A sequence of computational steps stored within a computer. It is the ability to hold an internally stored program that distinguishes a computer from any other information-handling machine (for example, an adding machine).

I/O (Input/Output)—Devices or processes used to get information to and from parts of a computer system.

IVANS—Organization that operates a value added network for the exchange of data between insurance organizations, especially between agencies and insurers. Also, the network operated by IVANS.

Job—A series of data processing steps or operations performed in succession as a unit of work to complete a given task.

"K"—A metric term for 1,000 (kilo). In computer applications, however, it means 1,024 bytes or characters. Used most often when stating memory capacity. ("128K" means 131,072 bytes of memory.)

Keypunch—A keyboard device that punches holes in a card to represent data.

LAN (Local Area Network)—A system for linking various computers and peripheral devices together over a relatively small geographic area through cable connections.

Laser Printer—A high-speed, non-impact printer that transfers toner powder to paper to produce images.

Lead Operator—The computer operator in charge of a shift, also called Shift Supervisor.

Leased Line—Same as Dedicated Line.

Line Printer—A high-speed printer that prints a line at a time versus a character at a time like a dot matrix or letter quality printer. Its speed is referred to in Lines Per Minute (e.g., 300 LPM).

Local—When applied to computer hardware, refers to those devices that are in the immediate vicinity of the central processing unit. Compare Remote.

Machine Language—The language that the computer actually "understands." All other languages must be reduced to this level before the computer can execute instructions.

Magnetic Core—An individual magnetic core is a tiny doughnut-shaped ring of ferrite capable of being magnetized in one or two states at any given moment. Thousands of these tiny rings were strung together to form primary storage in many third generation computers.

Mainframe—(1) A large computer. (2) An organization's main computer system.

Main Memory—Same as Primary Storage.

Maintenance Programming—Changing, that is, correcting or improving, existing programs. Compare Development Programming.

Management Information System—A group of people, a set of manuals, and data processing equipment that select, store, process, and retrieve data to reduce the uncertainty in decision making by yielding information for managers at the time they can most efficiently use it.

Matrix Printer—See Dot Matrix Printer.

Media—The means for storing computer readable data, including magnetic tapes, disks, and cards.

Megabyte—One million bytes (characters). Usually used when speaking of disk storage.

Microcomputer—Smallest type of data processing system available today; called personal computer (PC).

Microprocessor—A chip that contains complete processing circuitry.

Microprogramming—The technique of controlling various functions of the computer with pseudo-instructions already integrated into the computer circuits.

Minicomputer—A computer that is larger than a microcomputer. It is more expensive, may need special air conditioning or power, but has more storage capability.

Mnemonic Symbol—A symbol chosen to assist the human memory. For example, the symbol "prem" may represent "premium."

MODEM—A MODulation/DEModulation device that connects a computer to a telephone line in order to exchange information.

Mouse—A hand-held pointing device used to control the cursor or icon on a VDT.

Network—The communication vehicle for a computer equipped with the proper communication hardware to interface (send/receive) data with other interconnected computers at multiple locations.

Nonprocedural Language—A language that tells a computer what is to be accomplished. The compiler then determines how to do what has been asked. Compare Procedure-Oriented Language.

Object Program—Program in machine language. The programmer prepares a source program in an easy-to-use symbolic or procedure-oriented language and then assembles or compiles it into the object program.

Off-line—Computer operations performed without direct operator intervention. For example, printing invoices at night.

Off-Loading CPU—Removing functions normally performed by the central processing unit and putting them in some supporting device such as a front-end controller.

Online Processing—Processing which requires that computer terminals be attached to the computer, usually through telephone lines, and that they be able to access information in the computer as well as input information to the computer at any time desired by the terminal user. Normally, when any device is connected directly with the computer it is said to be online.

Operating System—The group of programs that control the physical operations of the computer and the movement of data between the parts of the system. This is the major component of systems software. A compiler is part of the operating system.

Operations—The group of people or department charged with the responsibility of physical maintenance, operation, and security of the computer itself.

Operator's Console—An input/output device used by the computer operator when specific instructions are needed to operate the computer itself.

Optical Character Reader—A computer input device that recognizes symbols printed on objects (for example, food cans at the grocery store) according to a standard coding scheme.

Output—Data disseminated by a computer to a device such as a CRT, printer, or disk.

Password—A code that grants a user access to a computer or to specific data or functions.

Peripherals—All computer hardware devices other than the central processing unit.

Plug-Compatible—Computer equipment produced to operate compatibly with IBM equipment. There are plug-compatible tape drives, disk drives, etc.

Polling—The process by which the central processing unit checks each terminal on the computer network sequentially to see if activity is desired by that terminal. This process must go on constantly while terminals are online and, of course, must proceed at a very high rate of speed.

Ports—Sockets used by computers to pass data to and from other devices. Serial ports pass information one "bit" at a time. Parallel ports pass multiple bits of information, usually one "byte" at a time.

Primary Storage—That part of the central processing unit designed for storage of programs and data which are being used by the computer at a given moment. New programs and data are constantly brought into primary storage as other programs and data are no longer needed.

Procedure-Oriented Language—A computer language that requires the programmer to specify exactly how the computer is to perform something. (For example, COBOL or BASIC).

Processor—Same as Central Processing Unit.

Program—A sequence of computational steps to be performed on data in order to perform a specific function.

Program Libraries—Collections of various programs.

Programmer—A person who designs, writes, and tests computer programs.

Programmer Analyst—A data processing job that combines the functions of a programmer with those of a systems analyst.

Prompt—A symbol or message that appears on a computer screen to convey an instruction to the user (e.g., the prompt CUST appears to tell the user to enter the customer name).

Protocols—Procedures used to transmit and receive information between communicating devices.

Query Languages—Computer languages that allow users to become more involved in the programming function than procedure-oriented languages do.

RAM (Random Access Memory)—Memory in the computer that holds application programs while they are being run. RAM is erasable so that when a program is finished, another program can be run using the same memory.

Random Access—Same as Direct Access.

Real-Time Processing—A specific type of online processing wherein the user has direct access to the computer and its files, and can use those files directly and immediately within the time required for an external event to occur. (For example, real-time processing provides immediate computer confirmation of a reservation.)

Remote—Those devices—usually terminals—that are removed from the immediate vicinity of the central processing unit. Compare Local.

Remote Processing—A type of service provided by vendors wherein terminals are installed at the user location and are connected by telephone lines to the vendor's computer.

Report Writers—Languages designed so that an end user can define certain parameters from which the report writer will then generate a program that will produce the desired report.

Response Time—In an interactive mode of operation, the lapsed time between the end of the input and the beginning of the output.

ROM (Read Only Memory)—Non-erasable memory used to store instructions that are always needed by the computer.

RPG (Report Program Generator)—A report writer language that is very popular in business.

Run—A sequence of computational steps to be performed on the data. Often used synonymously with program.

Semiconductor Memory—A type of computer memory utilizing silicon chips.

Sequential Access—An access method whereby individual data elements cannot be retrieved without reading a file from the beginning. Data stored on magnetic tape must be retrieved by sequential access. Compare Direct Access.

Service Bureau—A data processing vendor that normally provides contract systems analysis, programming, some data entry functions, and produces production runs.

Software—The programs needed to operate the computer system as distinguished from the physical machines. Compare Hardware.

Software House—A vendor that produces and markets software packages and provides contract programming services.

Source Code—Those statements a programmer writes in a particular language (COBOL, BASIC, etc.) to create an application program.

Special Purpose Computer—A computer designed for a special or limited purpose. Compare General Purpose Computer.

Spooler—A software package that uses buffer storage to control input/output and processing activities. Spooling allows one job to run while another is being printed.

Standalone Mode—A computer operating without the control or support of some other computer.

Structured Programming—Writing programs according to a set of rigid rules in order to decrease testing problems, increase productivity, and increase the readability of the resulting program.

Symbolic Language—High-level language developed as a solution to some of the problems associated with programming in machine language; utilizes mnemonic codes and macro instructions.

Synchronous—A type of data communication in which strings of characters are sent from one device to another within a specified length of time. Clocks in both devices must be "synchronized" in order to communicate. Most often used when large volumes of data must be transferred.

System—A computer and its associated peripheral devices (hardware) and programs (software). Also used for the combination of hardware and software designed to perform specific or multiple functions, such as an agency management system.

Systems Analyst—The person who specifies the scope and characteristics of programs and series of programs.

Systems Programming—Programming concerned with the internal operations of the computer as opposed to business problems. Compare Applications Programming.

Systems Software—Those programs that manage the internal operation of the computer rather than solve business problems. Compare Applications Software.

Tape Drive—The physical device that reads from and writes on magnetic tape.

Telecommunications—Data transfer over telephone or teletype lines from one terminal or processor to another. Basically the same as Data Communications.

Telecommuting (Electronic Cottage)—A work arrangement in which employees stay home all or most of the time and use computer terminals or microcomputers to process data and communicate the results to the office.

Teleprocessing—Data processing by means of a combination of computers and data communications facilities to process information to and from remote locations.

Teleprocessing Monitor—Software that operates under the control of the operating system and acts as a "mini-operating system" for those programs that are servicing interactive terminals in a computer network.

Terminal—A device attached to a computer that allows either input of data, output of data, or both. Usually consists of a VDT and keyboard.

Timesharing—A form of computer processing involving the simultaneous use of a number of computer terminals. Although many terminals may be served simultaneously, it appears to the terminal user that he or she is the only user of the computer.

Turnkey System—A system is said to be a "turnkey" if a single vendor provides the purchaser with hardware, software, and maintenance as a package.

Upgrading—Replacing a computer or computer system with more powerful or more sophisticated hardware and/or software.

User Friendly—A description applying to a system that is particularly easy for an operator to use. Characteristically, it provides for operator prompting and the use of mnemonics and reduces the need for reference to external documentation such as manuals or operator guides.

User-Oriented Languages—Languages that allow for more user involvement and control than that allowed by Procedure-Oriented Languages. Usually restricted in use to producing simple files and reports although their sophistication is increasing. Compare Fourth-Generation Languages.

Users—Usually refers to those people a computer serves; the data users rather than the computer operators. Same as end user.

Value Added Network—A network that, in addition to moving data from point to point, performs additional functions such as message batching and format conversion.

VDT (Video Display Terminal)—Same as CRT.

Verifying—In batch processing, the step of checking the validity of data already encoded onto punched cards or some other medium.

Virtual Memory—An operating system technique that allows auxiliary storage to be treated as if it were primary storage, effectively increasing the capacity of the central processing unit without the addition of physical storage in the CPU.

Window—One or more subdivisions of a VDT screen that can be expanded and contracted as needed by the user; a window allows display of information different from that on the rest of the screen.

Bibliography

Agency Automation Guide. Insurance Institute for Research, 1978.

American National Standard Vocabulary for Information Processing X3.12-170. American National Standards Institute, 1970.

Anderson, Robert J.; Hamburg, Eileen B.; McGahan, William F.; and Turner, Alan J. *Automation in Insurance.* Malvern, PA: Insurance Institute of America, 1988.

Athearn, James L. *Risk and Insurance.* St. Paul, MN: West Publishing Co., 1977.

Awad, Elias M. *Introduction to Computers in Business.* Englewood Cliffs, NJ: Prentice-Hall, Inc., 1977.

Biedma, Susan J. and Gatza, James. *Managing Automated Activities.* Malvern, PA: Insurance Institute of America, 1988.

Burch, John G., Jr. and Strater, Felix R., Jr. *Information Systems: Theory and Practice.* New York: John Wiley & Sons, 1974.

Canning, Richard G., ed. "Increasing Organizational Effectiveness." *EDP Analyzer,* May 1988, pp. 3-9.

_____. "Making Office Systems Pay Off." *EDP Analyzer,* February 1985, pp. 8-12.

_____. "Uncovering Strategic Systems." *EDP Analyzer,* October 1986, pp. 3-4, 6-7.

DeMarco, Tom and Lister, Timothy. *Peopleware: Productive Projects and Teams.* New York, NY: Dorset House Publishing Co. Inc., 1987.

The Diebold Group, ed. *Automatic Data Processing Handbook.* New York, NY: McGraw-Hill, 1977, pp. 5-6.

Friend, David. "Executive Information Systems: Successes and Failures, Insights and Misconceptions." *Journal of Information Systems Management,* Fall 1986, pp. 31-36.

Gantt, Michael D. "First Buyer: Beware of Great Expectations." *Computerworld,* 29 January 1979, p. S-5.

_____. "Up from Computerese." *Interface: Insurance Industry,* Winter 1978, p. 8.

Gunner, Holly and Gulden, Gary K. "Partnerships Between Executives and Information Professionals Speed Business Strategy Execution." *Information Management Review,* Spring 1986, pp. 12-18.

Huff, Sid L. "DSS Development: Promise and Practice." *Journal of Information Systems Management,* Fall 1986, pp. 9, 13.

Keen, Peter G. W. and Woodman, Lynda A. "What To Do with All Those Micros." *Harvard Business Review,* September-October 1984, pp. 142-150.

Kinderlehrer, Robert. *Handbook for Data Center Management*. Wellesley, MA: Q.E.D. Information Sciences, Inc., 1979.

King, John Leslie. "Centralized Versus Decentralized Computing." *Computing Surveys*, vol. 15, no. 4 (December 1983), pp. 319-348.

Martin, James. *An Information Systems Manifesto*. Englewood Cliffs, NJ: Prentice-Hall, Inc., 1984.

McCauley, John. "A Look at Interface." *Independent Agent*, September 1988, p. 77.

McFarlan, F. Warren and Nolan, Richard L., eds. *The Information Systems Handbook*. Homewood, IL: Dow Jones-Irwin, Inc., 1975.

McNurlin, Barbara Canning, ed. "Implementing a New Systems Architecture." *I/S Analyzer*, October 1988, pp. 6-11.

_____. "Preparing for Tomorrow's Systems Jobs." *I/S Analyzer*, May 1988, pp. 5-8.

Murdick, Robert G. and Ross, Joel E. *MIS in Action*. St. Paul, MN: West Publishing Co., 1977.

"The Other Dimension: Technology and the City of London—A Survey." *The Economist*, July 1985, p. City of London Survey 37.

Porter, Michael E. *Competitive Advantage*. New York: The Free Press, 1985.

Potential Health Hazards of Video Display Terminals. Cincinnati, OH: National Institute for Occupational Safety and Health (NIOSH), publication no. 81-129 (1981).

Quinn, James Brian. "Managing Innovation: Controlled Chaos." *Harvard Business Review*, May-June 1985, pp. 73-84.

Ralston, Anthony and Meek, C.L., eds. *Encyclopedia of Computer Science*. New York: Petrocelli/Charter, 1976.

Sanders, Donald H. *Computers in Business—An Introduction*. 3rd ed. New York: McGraw-Hill, 1975.

Senn, James A. *Information System in Management*. Belmont, CA: Wadsworth Publishing Co., 1978.

Stair, Ralph M., Jr. *Computers in Today's World*. Homewood, IL: Richard D. Irwin, Inc., 1986.

Webb, Bernard L.; Launie, J.J.; Rokes, Willis Park; and Baglini, Norman A. *Insurance Company Operations*. Vol I. Malvern, PA: American Institute for Property and Liability Underwriters, 1978.

Index

A

Access, direct, *13, 17*
  sequential, *13*
Accounting, internal need for
  computer, *93*
  need for computer, *106*
Accounts current system, *107*
Accounts payable system, *107*
ACORD, *122, 124*
  evolution of, *124*
  mission of, *124*
Adaptability, minicomputer, *36*
Addressing storage areas, *12*
Administrator, database, *59*
ADP (automatic data processing), *2*
Advantages of purchased software,
  64
Agencies, computers and, *96*
Agency automation, current status
  of, *108*
  objectives of, *107*
Agency automation assistance pro-
  grams, *114*
Agency/company interface, *107, 115*
  advantages of, *116*
Agency management system
  (AMS), *111*
  advantages of, *112*
    expandability, *113*
    greater control over costs, *113*
    greater control over data, *113*
    interface capability, *113*
ALU (arithmetic/logic unit), *10*
AMS (agency management system),
  111
Analog computers, definition of, *3*
Analyst, programmer, *59*
Applications programming, *58*

Applications software, *7, 25, 26*
  data management, *29*
  integrated packages, *29*
  spreadsheet, *28*
  word processing, *27*
Arithmetic functions, *8*
Arithmetic/logic unit (ALU), *10*
Artificial intelligence, *34*
Assembler, *21*
Associations, computers and, *96*
Automatic data processing (ADP), *2*
Automation, agency, objectives of,
  107
  being comfortable with, *69*
  evolution of insurance company,
    101
  insurance company objectives,
    98
  insurance industry, *89*
  objectives of, better decision
    making, *98*
    competitive advantage, *99*
    cost reduction, *98*
    displacement, *98*
    optimal use of information
      resources, *99*
    processing voluminous
      amounts of data, *98*
    traditional, *98*
Automation is a business issue, *108*
Auxiliary storage, *13*

B

Balance forward, *106*
Balancing user and IS responsibili-
  ties, *77*
Bar code readers, *15*
BASIC, *21, 24*
Batch interface, *118*

159